Master the Start

10 Steps To Get Out of Your Own Way and Create Your Dream Business

Erin Smith

Acknowledgements

To be able to share this book with the world holds so many emotions, but I first would never be able to do this without the love and support of my fiancé, J.J. Thank you for encouraging me and never letting me give up on my dreams. Thank you for pushing me to always be my best, and for keeping the family running and together while I pursue this giant dream.

To my Dad who taught me what entrepreneurship and hard work were all about. I am forever grateful for the work ethic I hold, and I know it's because of what you taught me growing up. To my Mom who always encouraged me to dream, to live a bigger life than what we had to keep writing. I will forever be grateful for you to always wanting me to dream.

And to my kids, T.J., and Lilly, you have inspired me so much in just the short time you've been a part of my life. Because of you I will never stop pursuing my dreams for the sole reason you will learn how to pursue yours. I love you to the moon and back and am so grateful every day for the gift I was given!

Table of Contents

Preface

Entrepreneurship was a word I would never have associated with myself. I grew up on a farm in Wisconsin and watched my dad work every single day of his life. Vacations were more stressful than fun because something always went wrong while we were gone. It made coming back home *more* work because of what needed fixing.

My dad is a workaholic (probably where I get it from). The day he stops working is the day he dies. As much as he loved farming and being on his own, he never wanted that life for us. My dad is a math whiz. When he graduated from the University of Wisconsin, he was offered an incredible job with a corporation in Milwaukee. He passed it up for the dream of owning his own farm and moved his family to the middle of nowhere. He has lived his dream, but I believe there was always something in the back of his head that made him wonder if life would have been easier had he taken that 'cush' job, instead.

For that reason, he pushed college and the idea of a 'safe' job onto me. Big time. There was never a question of if I would go to college or not. The real questions were where would I go and what would I major in. I loved writing, but I was especially good at math. I came across programming in college and thought it was a breeze. I did what any kid who had the idea of lots of money dangling in their face would do. I didn't think twice about doing what I love. Instead, I followed the money and majored in Management Information Systems.

Still, there was always an uneasiness for me throughout college. I knew I was going to graduate, get hired, and make a lot of money, but I wasn't sure of myself. I jumped between schools, played basketball for a year, quit, then drank a lot. By the time I was in my senior year, I was exhausted, burned out, and chalked it up to working too much. I gave no second thought to the fact that I was following a path that I didn't want to be on. I believed making money was the easy choice, and happiness and money couldn't go together.

Going to college and getting that 'pinnacle' job was almost too easy. I was home by 6:00 every night (versus having to go back to the barn at 5:00 each evening). I had weekends off. I even had Christmas off, a concept I hadn't experienced my entire life. I questioned why anyone would take two weeks of vacation a year when you could get paid for it later. I was so used to working so hard, that forty hours a week was already like a vacation for me. I was bored out of my mind and took a serving job at night.

A few years into my corporate journey, the company I was working for started to crumble. Fridays were no longer something to look forward to. They were something to dread. Each week found us in our cubicles at noon waiting for that phone call. It was the call that would end everything. The call to tell you they had let you go. It wasn't a matter of if; it was a matter of when. There was no good news either because if I didn't get the call, I was still sick from the stress. Plus there was always a friend to console who had gotten the call.

This caught me at a pretty bad time in my life. I was living with the concept that the money was going to go on forever. This was a whole new reality, something I wasn't prepared for. I was spending every single penny I made. All right, let's be honest: I was spending more than I was making. I was twenty-three with a mortgage and brand new car loan, and I had maybe $2000 in the bank. Not even enough to cover a month of bills should I have been the one to get that Friday phone call.

I was fortunate enough to jump ship before that happened. And I learned a very valuable lesson during that time. There is no safety in Corporate America. Even though I had new-found luxuries, I needed to start thinking of myself and creating my own destiny.

Was entrepreneurship the answer? Nope, I wasn't even thinking along those lines. That meant tech companies, huge investments, a restaurant, or some type of store. My mind was too small to think of myself as an entrepreneur. Yet, I knew passive income was now something I needed to create for myself. I needed to find a way to have money working for me instead of me constantly working for it. This was an entirely new concept for me since I had traded time for money all of my life.

I read the book 'Rich Dad, Poor Dad,' and my life was forever changed. I wasn't ready to jump ship from the corporate world or anything drastic, but I decided that I needed to figure out a way to make passive income. My journey technically started in stocks and real estate. My first step was researching the stock market, and I started putting money in to see what I could do. Before long, I was getting pretty awesome returns. In my early twenties, it became more fun for me to invest my money and watch it grow than to go buy frivolous things.

I went to real estate school at night and got my realtor's license. I saved up money to invest and started buying property across the country. I had some huge wins, and a few losses, and overall came out ahead. Weekends were spent looking for new properties, fixing up something I had purchased, or figuring out how I could invest more.

Was I now an entrepreneur? Nope, I wasn't ready to call myself that. I was just a corporate girl using my salary to do some side jobs.

When I was twenty-seven, I fell completely in love. He lived in Dallas, Texas; I lived in Scottsdale, Arizona. Although he eventually wanted to be in Arizona, he still had a few years until he finished his Ph.D. So I did what any crazy in love person would do, and bought a house half way across the country to be with him. Since I wasn't ready to say good-bye to my Scottsdale ways, I kept my house there, too, and spent a year living between the two cities.

When summer came, I told him (who is now my ex) if he had needed a job before I got there, then he needed to have a job while I was there. He went to the mall, found something at Sears, but he was completely miserable.

Randomly we started doing some research on dog care options, as I found myself with two dogs and no close friends to take them when we traveled. I rescued them from shelters, so boarding them wasn't an option, as I never wanted them to feel like I had abandoned them. It was then when we discovered the world of pet sitting.

My ex had the idea of taking on a few pet-sitting jobs with the initial intent being to pick up extra work over the summers so he could quit the mall job. I thought it seemed like a fun idea, and we even threw around the idea bringing in one other dog at a time and boarding them at our house too.

Having the real estate background, I knew the basics of setting up a business, and I registered and insured it. To announce our business to the world, we walked flyers in our neighborhood. Little did I know how much that tiny LLC would forever change my life.

Our first clients had a new baby and two rambunctious dogs. Unable to walk both of them at the same time, they hired us to walk them five days a week. I had no idea people paid this kind of money for services like this, especially when you could walk the dogs yourself. I had always considered that walking dogs were all part of being a dog owner and never ~~had~~ considered hiring anyone to do it for me. Needless to say, my eyes were definitely beginning to open to a whole new world.

Soon after starting, we realized this wasn't going to be just a summer gig. When fall came, my ex juggled school, and I juggled my corporate job while we ran this new business. I had no idea what I was doing. I felt my way through the business, thanks to books and Google.

The following year, we tried to find a pet sitter to take care of our dogs while we went to Hawaii to get married. After several companies never called us back, I had an ah-ha moment. If we weren't getting called back, who else wasn't? I found this huge opportunity, and I jumped on it. I ramped up marketing, taught myself Google AdWords, and started actually pushing this little side business.

By fall that year, we needed to hire our first employee. Again, having no idea what I was doing, I hired her, came home, and literally Googled 'How Do I Hire an Employee?'

Four years, twelve employees, the buy-out of two competitors, multiple years of six figures, and a divorce later, I sold the business.

Was I an entrepreneur now? Nope, still refused to label myself as that. It was just a pet sitting business, and I had not let go of my corporate job. I worked from home, took vacation time to work the business, and had to schedule the time to let my own dogs out during the holidays. I was living the entrepreneur life that my dad had lived. Although we did vacation, I never slept the night before. I was too busy making sure that everything was going to run okay without me. Every time we went anywhere, my first day was always spent catching up on sleep.

I moved to my next business, a mobile spray tanning company. I started with a partner, but after a few months, she was overwhelmed, and I bought her out. I was able to use my experience from the pet sitting business to get this one right from the start. Google AdWords was my savior. I also knew how to network, so I grew the business very quickly. In just nine months, I had seven employees, was located in six salons, had a mobile service that covered all of Dallas, and hit my first five-digit month.

I started contemplating about franchising this idea. I was ready to expand and thought I had it all figured out. I decided it was time to take that leap. It was a moment where I finally found the courage to cut that corporate umbilical cord. I told my boss my days were numbered. He begged me to stay, and I waivered, telling him I needed the weekend to think about it.

That weekend was grueling. A cheating boyfriend caused my star employee to unexpectedly pick up and move. That led me to a weekend of working from 7:00 AM to 8:00 PM just tanning people. Exhausted, knowing I had to hire a few more people, I decided to go back to the 'day job' a few more months while I got my business to where it required less of me in the day-to-day operations.

And then I was surprised with an umbilical cord of my own. I wasn't supposed to be able to get pregnant without medical intervention, but there I was a few evenings later, staring at a positive pregnancy test.

The next few months were like sitting in a car as it spun out of control with nothing I could do about it.

My pregnancy was high risk, so I had to cut back on my business. I stepped back from the salons and kept fewer employees on board. My goal during the pregnancy was to keep the business afloat and wait to see what would happen. I still knew how to market, and how to network, and knew that as soon as I was ready to put the gas pedal down again, I could make it grow.

Days were still long. I spent Thursdays and Fridays driving and working all day, and I still had my corporate job. Knowing I was going to have a newborn at home, I wanted to figure out something new. I wanted something that would keep my entrepreneurial juices flowing, but wouldn't require me to deal with so many employees or to be gone for long periods. As I got ready to put that business up for sale, I thought long and hard on what was next.

There were a few criteria that were really important to me. I didn't want investors. I had built my companies all on my terms. Sure, I had taken on some bank loans for my real estate, but everything else was boot strapping from my own funds. For me, it was important to continue to have that control.

I also wanted something that would make me finally cut the corporate cord. I wanted flexibility. I wanted something that would keep me home with my kids. I didn't want to send them to daycare, but I wasn't too proud to not ask for help either. I wanted it all and instead of thinking it was impossible, I created it.

That's when I started up The Starters Club.

Entrepreneur? Yep, I can finally say it's true.

As crazy as it may sound, I am finally to a point where I can call myself an entrepreneur. The term just isn't for the Steve Jobs or the Bill Gates of the world. It's for that person who can bring in any level of income. It's about creating your own destiny, and it doesn't have to be millions. Even if it's creating another $1000 for your family a month to have as fun money, you can still be an entrepreneur.

There are many who will never make the journey because they will never know what is possible, what they can do to bring money in, or believe they really can have flexibility. Many people will never believe they can have whatever it is they want. Even while I was *doing* it, there was still a part of me who didn't see all of the possibilities. It took me a long time to finally get there.

I can say I have no regrets in my life. Even the bad times taught me incredible lessons. If anything, I wish someone would have sat my twenty-one-year-old, newly college graduated butt down and told me about this whole world outside of Corporate America.

Let me back that up. I wish someone would have introduced me to this world outside of Corporate America long before that. I wish there had been someone who would have told me I could do it, and point out all of the possibilities. Instead, I took a few long years to figure it all out myself.

That's what this book is. I want to help you put it all together, learn how to believe in yourself, and to open your eyes to the possibilities. I want to show you that the life of work and making money is not black and white. There is a TON of gray area. And no matter what you want to do with your life, you can create it.

I spent so many years never knowing, never even thinking that I could have it in me. I watched others rise to success and told myself that it just wasn't going to happen. The one thing I never realized was that it was never going to happen as long as I sat back and never tried. I just wrote the label 'impossible' on everything and never tried.

Stick with me on this. I'll give you ideas, encouragement, and will help you open your eyes. No matter your past or your present, your future is yours for the creating. It's not up to your spouse, your children, your parents, or your friends. It is up to YOU to create it. So if that voice is now saying in your head: 'well, this chick just doesn't understand because....' Tell it to go away and just listen.

You can do this.

You just have to master the start.

Chapter 1

Get Yourself Ready To Start

When I initially began The Starters Club, it was created based upon a very simple premise. Because I had started and sold a few of my own businesses, people told me time and time again, how much they would love to start something. When I asked them why they didn't, it was always the same answer: 'Well, I just don't know *where* to start.'

Since I have always believed that the start was actually the easiest part, I put together a company with a sole mission that was going to be very simple; to help people start and build their businesses organically. And not necessarily the online businesses you see advertised on Facebook, but *any* business they truly wanted to build. My goal was to lay out the steps, piece by piece, and to give people the business fundamentals to get them exactly where they needed to be. I wanted to give more than just theories. I wanted to give them the actual steps from A to a real and profitable business.

However, I discovered that even with laying out those steps piece by piece, people still found excuses. Had I actually done the steps myself and handed them a business, packaged and ready to go, they still would have had excuses. They would think of every reason they could as to why they couldn't start it or run it themselves.

Time wasn't on their side. They had three kids and were juggling sporting events every weekend. They thought they missed this one crucial part to building their business, and they couldn't figure it out for themselves. They needed a little more money. You get my point. The list could be a book in and of its self.

Here's what I know. Label it however you want, it all comes down to one basic principle: self-sabotage.

During my time as an entrepreneur, I've learned one very simple concept. When it comes to setting priorities, we make the time for the things in life we find important. And that is the simple truth. Let me make sure I'm very clear on this because it's important. We don't suddenly find *extra* time for the things we consider important. We MAKE the time for them. We decide our kid's soccer future is way more important than our dreams. We decide one more episode of Real Housewives is just too good to not watch. We let another day go by without working on what we really want. We decide that looking at what our friends are doing on Facebook is far more interesting. We decide all these things are more important than building our own dream.

So before you try to tell me I don't understand because you don't have the time, I want you to really reconsider it. You have time. We're all gifted with the same amount of time in the day. It is all about what we choose to do with that time. By no means am I saying you need to put your kids' dreams aside for your own. What I am saying is that there is nothing wrong with finding a little balance. You need to remember how to make time for yourself.

So if it's simply a matter of finding the time to start and then starting, why is it that people *don't* start their business? Do they not really believe there is any value in it, or they don't make it a priority, and it's that simple? No, I don't believe that either.

Unfortunately, the biggest deterrent from us following our dreams and creating the life we want is the inner demons or voices that we live with every day. The ones that tell us we can't do it, or that we're not good enough. Or who do we think we are to believe that we can actually accomplish something? And who do we think we are to actually teach others how to do a specific thing or sell a certain item? They tell us that we need to be safe. That there is no way we can really create a life only we can imagine, or how we want it to be. Life is too hard to have that be true.

We fear putting ourselves out there because the idea of failing haunts us. What if we give something up that's good to attempt the great, and the great never happens? What if someone makes fun of us or tells us we're crazy? What if it ends up being really hard? I mean, why should we chance it when life right now is comfortable and easy?

So we listen to that voice and tell ourselves we'll take this chance when …. When we retire. When the kids are off to school. When we have just a little more money in the bank. We make up excuses one after another, watching those who are successful and thinking there is no way we could do the same thing.

I want to tell you one realization that finally hit home for me. It isn't that great entrepreneurs are that much smarter than you or me. It is that they simply had a belief sturdy enough to tell off the doubts that crept into their heads. They had a dream so big, that *not* going for it would cause them massive regrets that they just couldn't live with. They went for it. They had to, and what they didn't know they asked and figured it out.

I recently listened to a podcast with Jerry Seinfeld, and I loved his take on who becomes successful in comedy. He talked about how it wasn't the gifted, or the people who just had it. It was the people who wanted it more badly than the rest. The people who were willing to never give up and go for it day after day. Sure talent can help you, but it's tenacity that's going to carry you to where you want to go.

Here's another beautiful thing to know. There's not an entrepreneur in the world that hasn't had tremendous fear, and the realization that they don't know everything. It's the people who look at that as a challenge to push through, who become successful. It is the people who surrender to it, who don't. It's not that successful entrepreneurs don't have fears. They merely choose to acknowledge them, say thank you very much, and push through them.

I understand that paralyzed in fear feeling better than anyone because I lived it for a long time. I lived it for fourteen years. Yes, I started real estate companies, and then I started other companies. Even as I started making my own money, great money, and sold those businesses for a profit, I was still convinced I couldn't kick my corporate crutch. I made every excuse under the sun. Sure, I thought of myself as successful, but I wasn't successful *enough* to do it on my own. I told myself I needed a W2 to buy investment properties. Even while I was in the midst of all this, I never truly believed in a life outside of Corporate America. I told myself I needed more money, or that I needed a cushion, or that I needed insurance. You name it. I promise you, I have used every excuse in the book.

It all finally hit me like a ton of bricks one day when I realized I was angry, very angry. I was angry with myself for being scared all the time and not living my purpose in life. I was angry with everyone around me. I carried this massive chip on my shoulder. I hated everyone in my corporate job. If someone came to me with any issue, I wanted to explode.

Not only was I angry, but I was sad. I was sad that I looked forward to the end of the day because that meant it was one day closer to the weekend. I was sad because I watched year after year start with promising myself that this was the year I was going to do it. However, every year I was devastated to see December 31st hit with another set of promises I had made to myself unfulfilled. I had let myself down. Again.

Then I became depressed when I knew I should be grateful for what I had - a great job with good pay. I worked from home, and I could do it easily enough. So I got angry and depressed for feeling angry and depressed. I always struggled with the line of being grateful but wanting more.

That comfortable, safe place that I was so scared of leaving was causing me major misery. I realized that if I never took a chance and remained here in fear, I would probably hate myself forever. My anger at others was stemming from my anger at myself. I was scared, and I hated myself for it. I wasn't moving fast enough, and I was bitter about it. And everyone around me was suffering because of it, even my kids.

It was around that time when I came upon a quote that forever changed my life. It is 'your children will grow to be who you are, so be who you want them to be.'

I realized that I was setting my kids up to be angry and depressed people, when all I wanted for them was to live out their dreams. I could no longer tell them to do what I said and not as I did. I needed to change my life and show them what an example of living life to the fullest really meant.

It was at that point where I had enough, and I finally had to walk away. I was building The Starters Club, and things were starting to take off. I knew that if I didn't take this chance on myself, I would regret it for the rest of my life. I refused to let another year go by where I made a resolution to quit my job, setting myself up for never actually having it happen. I needed to be a better example for my kids. How could I tell them it was important to follow their heart when I was acting too scared to follow mine?

This was one of the hardest decisions I had to make. I was in the fortunate position that my kids' college funds were already taken care of because of my diligence in investing. I agonized over the possibility of having to dip into that fund to follow my own dreams. I cried many times over the question: Would I be jeopardizing my kids' future for my own happiness?

On the other hand, I also had to ask myself this: But what happens if I can give them an even better life?

I also saw what you've seen, other people making money, becoming successful, and I had to wonder whether it was all simply too good to be true. Or instead of being excited that I could do it too, I would tell myself I couldn't. I talked myself out of believing I could create the life I truly wanted. I talked myself out of believing I was worth it. I told myself it must be too good to be true. My inner voice of 'who the hell are you to do this?' kept creeping into my mind time and time again.

I finally had to take a chance and told that inner voice off. I can't tell you that the voice never comes back. In fact, it comes back pretty much daily. However, when you're living in alignment with what you should be doing, moving forward becomes easier, and letting that voice get the best of you becomes harder.

I haven't looked back, and I'm learning that it really is all possible, and it isn't too good to be true. It is true. My hope is that I can bring you with me. I wake up each morning doing exactly what I want to do. I no longer have to spend hours on spreadsheets that never really mattered. I no longer have to sit in meetings that are just prepping for other meetings about meetings. And the best part is that I no longer have to talk to other people who are completely miserable about their life. I'm sure you may have just one or two of those at your office.

There are pure bonuses to this too, where I get to take breaks during the day to pick up my kids from school and do fun things like making play-doh. My calendar belongs to me and no one else.

The part that you think is really hard, the part that people get most tripped up about, is the easy part. There isn't an entrepreneur in the world who started out knowing everything. Entrepreneurship is a journey. You're going to mess up. You're not going to be perfect, and you're going to get the opportunity to keep going and to do better. And you're going to learn. You're going to learn a lot. I promise you, within a solid month of entrepreneurship, you'll be amazed at how much you've already learned.

We are in an age where more and more people are sharing their knowledge. They understand the importance of teaching others, rather than hoarding everything they know. Add Google, and there's almost nothing that isn't at your fingertips when it comes to learning. You don't have to haul yourself to networking event after networking event just to meet people. Social media allows you to connect with pretty much anyone you would ever want, worldwide!

So here is the first thing I want you to do to help you believe in yourself a little more. When you think of one question that's tripping you up when it comes to being an entrepreneur, put down this book and Google that question. It is true that I did this in my first company. I did this a lot. Like I mentioned earlier, I used Google to hire my first employee. I also used it to help me learn how to build my first website, and I used it to learn Google AdWords. I knew none of these things when I started, but I just kept learning along the way.

By no means am I saying that everything you find on Google is always right, but it is certainly going to take you one step closer to the answer.

Continue to take a new step like that every day, day after day, and suddenly you're leaps and bounds closer to where you need to be. It just takes putting one foot in front of the other. Even if you are setting aside only an hour a day to work on your business, you'll be making massive progress. I recently had Steven Daar on my podcast and he broke it down like this; if you take just one positive step every day, in one year, you've taken 365 steps towards bettering your business. One step may not even take an hour. It could be something crazy easy that takes just five minutes!

Now that you have one pressing question answered, what is your excuse? Your family? I'm here to tell you, you are doing them a disservice by staying stuck where you are. It is harsh, but it's true. We make the excuses that our kids need us, or we can't pursue our happiness because, heaven forbid, we will end up making them miserable.

What if I told you that one of your jobs as a parent is to find your happiness, too? I'm not telling you to get something going where you are away from them 12 hours a day. I'm simply telling you that living your passion and following your dreams are part of your job as a parent. When it comes down to it, isn't that ultimately what you want for your children? Instead of just being comfortable, be a living example for them. I don't care who you are. We all have something that makes us tick, and I believe it's our jobs as human beings to find that and to make it a reality.

I also had a great friend, Chandra Achberger, tell me something that hit home as well: it is our job to teach others what we know. If we don't follow through with doing that, we are doing others and ourselves a disservice. So if you can't find it in you to do this for yourself, do it for the people you are letting down by not doing it. Any time I feel like quitting, this is one big thing that keeps me going. There will always be someone who doesn't know all of what you have learned, who you can teach. Just remember that if there is something you happen to know a lot about, you should be sharing it with the world. Even if you're only at a level of four of knowledge (on a scale of ten), there are people at a one, two and three that you can teach.

There is no greater time than now to start, and I mean that with every ounce of my soul. I started building the concept to my third business when my second baby was a newborn. Yes, it took a while for it to get off the ground, and yes, it was much harder to start than when I didn't have kids. But I started. I stumbled along, but I started. I can't grow at the rate I could without kids, but I'm still growing. I mean it when I say anything is possible.

There is a moment in your life when you have to tell yourself that you want more than good and that life isn't worth living if it's just good. You have to be grateful for what you have. However, you need to believe that there is something more amazing on the other side, and that's what you want, and that you deserve it and believe you can have it.

I went to a conference not too long ago where I was fortunate to see Jack Canfield speak. He ended his speech with four words I will never forget: 'My life is magical.' Magical. That word hit me hard. That has clung to my heart, and I won't stop until I can say the same thing about my life. I believe there isn't a single one of us who shouldn't strive for magical.

Now is your time. So let's figure out how to make you an entrepreneur.

Chapter 2

Prep Yourself for Entrepreneurship

There are a few things about entrepreneurship that I need to prepare you for. I'm not telling you this so you'll get discouraged and walk away. I want you to be ready for when it comes. It isn't hard, but you'll probably have a hardship or two before you are well on your way to massive success.

We are not up to the actual steps of starting your business, yet. Those will come later. This is about getting you, no matter who you are, no matter what your background, to wrap your mind around what it takes to become an entrepreneur. This is about letting you know deep down that you can do this.

Let's begin with one of the first things you're going to have to deal with, haters. Be warned, there are going to be people - and unfortunately, some of those really close to you - who are going to tell you that you can't. You are probably going to run into a few more than just two or three. Your friends or family might tell you that you are crazy. You will have others telling you it is all too good to be true.

Heck, you may also find that you are your own worst enemy with that whole inner voice talk we discussed earlier.

Here are straight-up reasons for that. First, especially with family, it is their job to keep you safe. So the last thing they want to see is for you to fail. Second, they are too afraid to do it themselves, so putting others down makes them feel better about their decisions. Third, they are utterly miserable, and the last thing they want is to see you accomplish something you've set your mind to. It is rather sad, but it's true. If they start to get to you, then ask yourself one simple question. Ask yourself if these people, the people who are too scared to follow their own dreams, are going to be the people who you let hold you back from yours.

When I graduated from college, two of my friends and I decided that if we didn't get out of Wisconsin then, we would never leave. I love Wisconsin, but winter and I don't agree with each other. I had no job, a new car loan, and $1500 in my bank account. I felt rich, and I had this idea that when I showed up in Arizona people would be begging me for a job because I had heard they loved people from the Midwest due to their work ethic. My mom and dad didn't have the same vision and told me over and over how it was a really bad idea.

I refused to believe it. There was just something that I still can't explain to this day that was telling me that Arizona was where I needed to be. Call it faith, or call it complete naiveté and stupidity, but I knew I had to leave. I packed all of my belongings in my newly purchased GMC Jimmy and headed to Arizona.

When I hit Iowa, my 'new' car's 'Check Engine Light' appeared, which led to a day delay in a dealership's service department in the middle of Iowa. They couldn't figure out what was wrong. So I made another appointment in Nebraska. The only problem was the service guy said it would be a few days before he could get me in. I had an interview in Arizona just a few days away, and time was not on my side. He convinced me I might as well keep driving, and take it all the way to Arizona.

Believe me, looking back, I realize what a complete idiot I was. The safe person I am now would never have taken an obviously broken car half way across the country. But I had faith. It is absolutely amazing what you can do when you believe that nothing can go wrong.

I made it to Arizona and ended up needing to have my entire transmission replaced. Luckily, it was all under warranty, and I didn't have to wipe through my savings.

I also made it in time for my first interview. However, I found that people were not dying to hire me as I had thought. As I got further into it, I learned this was all going to be just a bit harder than I originally planned. I picked up a serving job right away to help cover the bills while I continued to search for a job.

Four months in my parents were telling me I should give this up and move back home. I refused to believe them and just kept my eye on the bigger picture. Five months in, and still no 'real' job, I started to waiver and consider coming home.

Six months in, I sat in an office at Anderson Consulting, now called Accenture. They offered me a job and asked me for my salary requirements. I took a deep breath and uttered a number I could never imagine being paid for one job: $35,000. The guy shrugged and nonchalantly said 'well the position pays $42,000'. I thought I was going to have a heart attack.

Moving to Arizona ended up being one of the best decisions I ever could have made in my life. I often find myself wishing my thirty-seven-year old self could find even half of that 20-something courage so naturally. It is amazing that the longer life goes on, the deeper you have to dig for the courage. I guess you could say it's because more is at stake, but it is important that we never lose it.

When you believe this - you know in every ounce of your soul that not only is it going to work, but that it has to work - then that is all that matters. You may have to convince people, but that's okay. As Paulo Coelho writes in 'The Alchemist,' *When you possess great treasures with you, and try to tell others of them, seldom are they believed. (135)*' You can't let them talk you down. If making leaps of faith were truly easy, then everyone would do it. There would be not one person miserable and unhappy in this world. It clearly doesn't work that way.

The next nugget you need to know about entrepreneurship is that it isn't easy. I know, I know, you see it all the time in advertisements, how all you need is a website, or simply make the intention and put it out the world, and people start magically lining up.

I wish I could tell you all you need is an idea and one step forward, but unfortunately it doesn't work that way. If it did, then everyone and their mom would be an entrepreneur. The only place where the 'if you build it, they will come' mentality worked was in *Field of Dreams.*

Again, I'm not saying any of this to discourage you; to make you put down this book with the conclusion that your dream is over. I'm telling you this to set realistic expectations. Even though it isn't easy, it is very possible. It takes a ton of tenacity, and a ton of hard work, but if you are willing to put that in, you will be thrilled with the results.

I love how Brendon Burchard put it at a conference I recently attended. It's not that it's hard, it's simple steps, but there happens to be a lot of them. This is what I have found for every business that I've started. You have to put a lot of moving parts together to make it all happen, and it's easy to get overwhelmed by those parts and label it all as 'hard.' When you break it all down, though, it's simply putting one foot in front of the other.

You will learn to wear a lot of hats, but the point is you will learn. You will learn how to juggle, and how to prioritize, but if you keep reminding yourself it is all simply putting one foot in front of the other, you are going to get there. I doubt you will have people dying to hand you money as soon as you open your doors, but you are going to get there.

Stop watching everyone else do it and thinking that you can't because they are better at this than you. Or they are luckier than you, or they don't understand why you can't start, or they have the money to risk, and you don't. In fact, stop thinking money is your biggest obstacle. There are so many ways you can bootstrap, which is using your own resources to build your business by continually putting in what you are making. You can even get investors. Before you tell me I'm crazy, I have one question. Have you even started researching the possibilities?

The third nugget that you need to know about entrepreneurship is there is nothing that's going to help your confidence more than surrounding yourself with other entrepreneurs. As someone who has experienced corporate networking events and entrepreneur networking events, I can tell you there is such a major difference. Entrepreneurs will lift you up. When your family is telling you, you're crazy; entrepreneurs will swap crazy stories with you.

Entrepreneurship can be a very lonely lifestyle. Learning to surround yourself with peers and mentors will not only help your business, but it will also help you personally. Find local networking events. Find groups on Facebook and Communities on Google+ filled with entrepreneurs (you can even get specific about the type of entrepreneur). Label yourself as an entrepreneur and put yourself out there. Find someone who has already been through it and take them out to lunch for advice.

You simply have to ask. Don't shy away because you don't believe you're worthy, or you feel like they're not going to help you. If they do say no, then ask someone else.

Surrounding yourself with entrepreneurs will change your life. Where corporate people tend to talk down about their day, entrepreneurs share ideas and are excited. Be in tune to this if you are still in Corporate America. Start noticing the misery people are living with every day, and vow to not be one of them. On the flip side, entrepreneurs are typically excited to share what they have learned and to help others around them.

Even if you don't have a single detail of your business put together, look for those local groups and groups on Facebook and Google+ now. There is nothing wrong with showing up to a networking group, to say you're thinking about starting a business and that you want to start meeting people. I see people do this quite a bit, and other entrepreneurs are always willing to give advice and share ideas.

It doesn't matter about your current financial situation. It doesn't matter where you live. It doesn't matter what your business idea is. I'm telling you that if you really want this, and you believe in yourself, then your life and your career are for the creating. Not the taking, but for the creating. You can choose to live a life you want. You can make money doing truly anything that you can put your mind to, as long as there is some sort of need.

The question you have to ask yourself is how bad do you want to live the life of your dreams? If the answer is really bad, then it's time to move on to the next chapter. If the answer is anything less than that, then entrepreneurship may not be for you. Giving up is far easier than seeing it through to the end. And notice I'm not asking you if you think it's possible. I'm asking how badly you want it. Because no matter how crazy your dream is, anything is possible.

Chapter 3

What Do You Create A Business Around?

We live in a world where anyone can make money doing pretty much anything they set their mind to. Couple this with belief in yourself to start a business and the question then becomes how do you determine exactly what you want to do for a living?

I hear this all of the time from my clients. So many of them like the idea of kicking the corporate crutch and starting their own business, but they're completely lost over what they would do.

I used to stumble over this myself. Coming from the corporate world, my view of businesses was quite skewed. I thought either I had to create a brick and mortar business where I sold a specific product, start a restaurant or bar, or create a tech business, which would require investors. None of these things appealed to me, so I basically shut off the possibility of entrepreneurship.

When you hear the word entrepreneur, too many of us automatically assume it entails expensive overhead, employees, and crazy costs to get started. However, you can create a business (which allows you to call yourself an entrepreneur) where you're setting your own hours, doing what you want to do, and still have enough money coming in to survive.

When figuring out what it really is you can do for a business, the first thing you need to look for is what you're passionate about. Some people may know already. However, I have found that most people don't. If we did then 'The Purpose Driven Life' wouldn't have become a best seller. I've found way too many people who really don't understand what their passion is. On the other end of the spectrum, some people will chase anything that makes money and try to forge their passion into that.

The next question then is: 'Well, how do I know what *my* passion is?' A simplified answer would be it's what makes you tick. If you had just a few hours a week to do anything you wanted, and money didn't matter, what would you do? (I'm talking about something fulfilling - mind growing, not mind numbing work. Vegging out in front of the television or Facebook doesn't count.) Is there something you've always wanted to learn to do, but you never made the time? Is there something you love to work on, but you put it on the back burner because you think it's merely a hobby?

I may make it sound easy to put together. I know in reality it's not. We have made ourselves believe that working day in and day out is what life needs to be about. We don't feel like we deserve to do what we love. I've talked to countless people who say they're not sure what they're passionate about. They're not sure what they would do if they could make money doing anything they could possibly dream of.

I can say that I didn't really start paying attention to my own passions until I was in my thirties. I was going through a divorce, and was seeking a lot of help during that time. Long story short, my ex-husband had me convinced that I was pretty crazy. He told me I needed to see a therapist for him to stay with me. As crappy a thing as it was for him to do, it ended up being one of the best things that ever happened to me.

Insert my therapist who queued me into something pretty amazing. First, he made me analyze the things that I did while I was growing up, but didn't exactly love doing. One of them was basketball. It was my dad who really wanted me to play, and I kept convincing myself that I loved the sport too. It was finally at the end of my freshman season in college, when I was able to admit to myself that I wasn't doing it for me, and walked away from it. I wish I could say it was an easy choice for that time in my life. Instead, I lived with massive guilt over the decision for many years after.

Once I could finally let that guilt go (which by the way was followed by a four hour cry fest), I was able to tell myself it was okay for me to not love things that I forced myself to do in my twenties. A great example of that was my corporate job. I never could understand why I was so miserable in the corporate world, and I kept telling myself I needed to suck it up and work. Talking to that therapist allowed me to actually feel the misery that I was feeling in my job. And the beautiful thing about feeling that misery - it let me realize I wasn't all that crazy. It just meant I didn't love my job. It wasn't my thing, and I shouldn't feel crazy for wanting to run from work every day as fast as I could.

For the first time in my life, I gave myself permission to be miserable. But with that discovery came the responsibility to not allow myself to remain there any longer. I had to make a change.

One of the oddest phenomenas in this whole experience was that when I was in decision making mode, I was now able to ask myself the question, which I had never asked myself before: "Will this make me happy?" *Happy?!* Happy didn't put food on the table. Happy didn't pay the bills. I had always thought happy was something to feel outside of work, and dealing with it was more the work related feeling. Understanding the importance of that question changed everything for me.

It was time to discover what I truly loved. My therapist told me to think back to when I was a child, to remember when money and time didn't matter. Remember when I had all I ever needed, and time took *forever*? What did I do? My first choice was writing. I loved to write. I wrote every day, stories and novels, you name it. As I got older I pushed it back, and the more I pushed it off, the more creativity seeped away. By the time I had hit my thirties, I had no more ideas, no more vision for stories, just dead end wishes, and resolutions that I would finish my books, secretly knowing it wasn't ever going to happen.

I had gone from ideas for stories in books coming to me, one after another, to not thinking about it all. It broke my heart when I realized that had happened. Creativity is one of those things that it so vital for our happiness, yet it is the first thing we let go. Unfortunately, creativity doesn't just appear. It's something we cultivate. The loss of creativity equates to a loss of new ideas. I'm not exaggerating when I say my creativity went completely away. I think that so many people end up miserable because they forget to be creative. It's like what I felt about happiness, they feel that creativity doesn't pay the bills.

Another question to ask yourself is: What would the child version of yourself want for you? Too often we discount those things we loved to do as a child because, well, we were just kids. We had no idea how to be realistic. We simply did things. But if we look back, we'll have some amazing insight on what makes us tick.

When we are kids, we truly do what we *want* to. Money isn't an issue, and at that moment in our lives, we're invincible. We have all the time in the world and we spend it doing what we enjoy. We play, and we use our imaginations. We can even be super heroes. Anything is possible.

As you try to figure out what it is you're passionate about, first ask yourself if there is something from your childhood that you would love to do again. Would you love to pick up a pen or a paintbrush? Maybe you were obsessed with baseball. Your opportunity for a pro career might be gone, but can you do something else with it? Is there something that just came naturally to you? Don't discount it because it may feel silly. Go with it. Do it again. Even if it's just an hour a week, and see where it takes you.

If you can't think of anything that you loved as a child, then here's another question: 'What are you curious about?'

Not that just because you're curious about it, you have to up and make a living doing it. That's what fostering your curiosity is all about: finding out what you truly love, and finding out what really makes you happy. Then you can take that and see if it is something you want to pursue taking to another level.

Here's an example of how this helped me with a huge decision in my life. One of my major passions is baking. I love it! If I had all the time in the world, I would bake cakes and cookies every day. That love of baking harbored a dream. I had a big vision for a new concept bakery. I even started scoping out property in certain areas of Dallas and really started to consider how I could make it happen.

Even as I laid the groundwork, I knew if I was going to take this seriously, I needed to work on my decorating and presentation skills. As awesome as I was at baking, the final product never seemed to look quite as good as it tasted.

I took courses so I could up my game. My first class was something Michael's offered, but it was boring, and I grew impatient with it very quickly. I decided to take it to an entirely new level, and I took courses and started learning from some of the best in the industry. I got a little over my head when in my very first class. I was the only one who didn't own a cake shop. When we were told to crumb coat our cakes, I had to watch what everyone else was doing because I had no idea what crumb coating meant.

In exploring my love of baking and my curiosity in the possibilities, the classes taught me a ton. One thing being the time commitment required to make a cake look amazing. Add that to all I was learning about the world of bakeries and cake decorating, I realized in a hurry this venture was not going to be for me. I knew if I made a career out of this, the stress would get the better of me, and before long, I wouldn't be happy with the business.

I did not lose my love for baking. In fact, I still get incredibly excited for my kids' birthdays because I love creating some pretty pimped out cakes. What I have moved on from is that little voice in the back of my head saying maybe I want to own a bakery. I fostered that idea, learned more about it, and ultimately determined my time is better spent elsewhere. Those business plans have been sent to the 'not going to happen' pile.

Was that a complete waste of time and money? Heck, no! What's awesome about exploration is that now I know. I won't live with regrets wondering if maybe I should have opened a bakery. I tried, and I learned it just wasn't for me. With no regrets, I moved onto the next thing that interested me.

So don't stress because you don't yet have this deep-desire passion about what you want to do for the rest of your life. At least start seeing what piques your interest. You don't have to start building your business right now, but you can at least start laying out a path toward figuring out what you want to do, and making a plan around it.

I have a client who was really struggling with this whole idea of passion and what it meant. Although she knew she was really getting sick of the corporate job, she never thought of herself as an entrepreneur. Plus she had no idea what she even wanted to do in place of it. Instead of stressing about it, I told her to simply start earnestly seeking clarity.

At this time, I was in the process of putting together an online magazine, and I knew she was trying to learn as much about the online world as she could. Since I was just learning the magazine thing myself, I asked her if she wanted to help. I knew an extra set of eyes is always beneficial, and I knew she could use the knowledge.

The weird thing is that by me asking her if she wanted to help with an online magazine, it triggered memories she had about creating a magazine almost thirteen years prior with some friends. What's crazier is because of how far technology has come, the original idea was ten times easier to take to create and build now than it had been when they were originally working on it. It was the logistics of it all that forced them to set it aside, yet here she was all that time later, ready to move forward with the idea again.

What is really amazing is that now because of that one step, she has a business that is growing, and she is making plans to eventually move away from her corporate job. You can't even say that she went from an idea to a business because for a while she didn't even know she had the idea. Sometimes all it takes is for us to open our minds to the possibilities and start looking at life just a little differently.

Think five years back to what you loved; what made you excited. If five years doesn't do much, then go a little deeper (you don't *have* to make it all the way back to childhood). Was there some idea that maybe you and your college roommates got excited about? Was there something you thought to yourself 'if only there was a business that did this' but you set aside the idea for whatever reason? Has there been anything that piqued your interest, but you buried it because life just got the best of you?

My client is pushing forward, having revived her dream, and making it that much better now that technology can allow her to create and build it far easier. It's moments like hers that keep me pushing with this message because, you see, anyone - and I mean ANYONE - can make a living doing what they love. All it takes is a passion. The only requirement of you is to move in a direction where you can discover what that is.

I don't believe we give our passions nearly enough credit. We tend to believe sure, we like something, but everyone likes that. We don't understand that what makes us excited doesn't make everyone else excited. We are all uniquely different.

My desire to create? It wasn't just through stories. I managed to harness inspiration into a passion for creating businesses. But! I had assumed because it was easy for me to take an idea, figure it out, and run with it, everyone else must be able to do the same thing. I realized later it was a gift which fueled a passion. This entire revelation was truly life changing for me.

I thought I must be engineer material when I discovered I was pretty good at coding in high school. Fast-forward four years, when I discovered that I didn't like spending hours scouring pages of code for a missing period that was causing an error. Just because I could do an engineer's job, didn't mean I should be one, so I nixed it as a possibility.

I think sometimes we put the bad moments in the category of 'Unhappiness We Have to Live With.' The problem comes when we never do anything about the unhappiness or bad moments.

I also believe too many times we chalk up our negative moments to having a bad day, or being tired, etc. We go to a job and work because we feel like we have to even though it doesn't ignite us or make us excited. We tell ourselves to just 'suck it up' and live with it.

I'm embarrassed to say this, but I used to be proud of the fact that I could do my job in my sleep. How sad is that? I never pushed myself to grow; I did the same work day in and day out. Sure there was a different client, and maybe a new business to learn, but when it came down to it, it was all the same. That was a very sad reality to take in.

I have made no secret of when it was time to pick a major in college, I went with the most money for the smallest effort route. I knew if I majored in Management Information Systems, I could get a job easily, and I could make great money. I could be, what I felt at the time was successful.

During my senior year we had to do a project where we researched the happenings in our industry (M.I.S.), and give a presentation about it. I can remember this moment so clearly, almost fifteen years later. These guys in my class did their presentation about how online banking was going to be an amazing phenomenon (yes, I understand how much I'm dating myself by sharing this story with you).

Their presentation showed a guy rushing to the bank on a Saturday and because he got there after noon, he wasn't able to deposit a check, and therefore was going to be out of cash for the whole weekend. (For you younger ones reading, this is not fiction. This actually used to happen to us. Just think of a poor college kid unable to get cash for beer for the weekend. Credit cards weren't as easy to come by as they are now either.)

As I watched their entire presentation, and listened as they talked about banking going online, I was amazed. First to learn about it; I was literally seeing this for the first time. Second, that they actually knew this trend was happening. When each class was over, I did go home and do my homework. However, once it was finished, I closed my books and never looked at them again. I never read extra books or industry magazines. I really didn't care about it.

They, on the other hand, were interested in what we were learning. So much so, they had done research outside of our classroom work to learn how the industry was changing.

This should have been an insanely profound moment for me. One where I marched down to the administration office and changed my major right there on the spot. Sure, I felt a little icky inside, that this was all new to me. This was an industry I was about to dedicate my entire life to. Instead of letting it be a moment that forever changed my life, I shrugged it off, telling myself I was busy and didn't have time to research stuff like this. They obviously must have had more free time than I did. At least that's how I convinced myself.

It was probably six years later when I truly started to understand my misery. It was another eight years, when I finally let myself believe I could take matters into my own hands.

I could give countless examples of passion and curiosity, but I'll just give one more. Let's talk about cooking again. I happen to be a huge fan of Top Chef. I am always intrigued when I watch what these people come up with. Now as intrigued as I am, and with how much I love to bake and cook (all via recipes), I still have no desire to go to school and learn what these people know.

Their imagination and creativity are absolutely fascinating to me. If you handed me a piece of bacon, a bottle of ketchup, and a loaf of bread, I would fry the bacon, put it on the bread and throw some ketchup over it. That is the extent of my creativity in the kitchen.

These people, on the other hand, would create some remarkable masterpiece that I could never imagine.

That right there is passion. They *love* doing what they do. They've spent the majority of their life learning their craft. They'll probably never be finished learning it. Yet, instead of discouraging them, it drives them, it gets them up every morning. Every day they're excited about the opportunity to learn more and create new masterpieces. I would be willing to bet that none of these chefs have ever said that they could do their jobs in their sleep.

Do you see what it means to find passion? And ways you can figure it out if you haven't put it all together quite yet?

Let me take a step back, and say that I completely understand entrepreneurship isn't for everyone. In no way am I saying that in order to be happy, you have to own your own business. What I *am* saying, is that in order to be happy you should be living your passion, and what you were put here on this earth to do. More common than not, the corporate lifestyle doesn't allow for that. You're spending many hours of your life working on someone else's terms, building their dreams, and doing what *they* want you do, not what you want to do.

So go out and start thinking about what makes you happy. The next time you have a free hour, just spend it doing something you enjoy. If something gets you even the slightest bit excited, don't take it for granted. Instead, remember it and revisit it to see how much you actually enjoy doing it. Start being open to the possibilities, and look at life just a little differently.

You will begin to learn what you enjoy doing, and what you may want to do for a business.

Chapter 4

Understanding Business Models

We are in a time in our lives, where I truly feel the sky is the limit. If you don't believe me, just take a quick moment and check out this website:

http://www.youtube.com/user/DisneyCollectorBR

Now you may be thinking: why in the world would she send me to this horribly boring YouTube Channel? I have not verified this information, but I did learn from a news channel, the YouTubers who run this channel make over $5,000,000 a year. Yes, I have the commas and all the zeros right, 5 million dollars! I guess kids are mesmerized by it, and the money comes from advertisements.

How can you watch this channel and still look me in the eyes and tell me you can't make money doing what you love? You can absolutely make money doing anything you want to (and make it all legally).

Still need convincing? Let me give you some specific examples of how money could be made from something most people would consider to be only a hobby: hunting. Let me just say as a side note that as I finalize this book, the Cecil the Lion issue is in the forefront of the news, along with illegal hunting. However, that type of hunting isn't what I am referring to.

Even if you are an animal lover, stick with me. I by no means am a hunter, but I do have a good reason for bringing this up. I grew up in the middle of nowhere Wisconsin where hunting was a very big deal. It was such a big deal that schools shut down for the first week of deer season. It is something I never got into, but my dad did, big time, and so I was forced to live and breathe it for many months every year.

I started thinking about this hobby of his, and should he retire, could he make money doing things related to hunting? The reason this particular topic is fresh on my mind is because I recently had a conversation with my father about what we imagined heaven to be like. I said how I felt we get to hang out with our loved ones, and I hoped dogs would be there, too. My dad told me that he believes we will also be able to do the things up there that brought us joy here on earth. For him, one of those things is hunting. Yes, the man loves hunting so much that his version of heaven has an endless opportunity to hunt.

After our conversation, I was considering examples for this book and decided hunting was the perfect hobby to use. Who could possibly make a living around hunting?

So if you still think it's a crazy idea to consider a beloved hobby for making money, observe. In just a few short minutes, I was able to come up with six examples:

1. Create a Blog about hunting. You could approach it several different ways. You could have a very specific niche and talk about only one sport; deer season, for example. Or you could even get more specific and differentiate between bow hunting and gun hunting. (Seriously, I sometimes amaze myself with how much I know about hunting when I've never done it in my life.) Your blog could become the place hunting enthusiasts come to check out stories, find the latest and greatest supplies, etc. Then from this one blog, here are a few ways you could make money:

   a. Advertisements - Once you drive enough traffic to your site, companies will pay you for that exposure. That doesn't happen overnight, but with diligent work, it will happen.

   b. Product Reviews and Sales – You could review certain products that make your life easier as a hunter, and then write/blog about how they have done exactly that. These companies could pay you to review their products, give you free products, or you could take a percentage of what you sell via affiliate links.

2. You could create a product that makes your life as a hunter easier. Yes, this may take a little more capital, but Duck Dynasty comes to mind. Granted, they are an extreme situation, but it truly is proof that the sky is the limit. I love the story how Phil Robertson believed in his duck call and worked as a fisherman while he tried to get his call to the market. One new duck call and a ton of hustle created that entire empire, and it was all based around hunting. They had a lot of money long before they become the phenomenon they are now.

Again, this isn't going to happen overnight. You're not going to develop something and within a few months, you are raking in millions. However, you could build a website to sell the product yourself, or you could work with retailers and wholesale to sell them for you. Sure, it's going to take some research and work, but once again, nothing that is of value comes easy.

3. You could create a company that offers training and boarding for hunting dogs. I have harped on my dad for many, many years about this one. He is a pro when it comes to training hunting dogs. Boarding facilities charge thousands of dollars to train dogs. The great thing about it is, (I'm totally bragging on my father) his dogs run circles around the dogs that have been trained by the expensive facilities.

My point isn't just to brag, but to show that if you have grown up living and breathing a specific thing, then you probably know a lot more about it than people who are just trying to get in on it. Dog training is one I'm thinking of for my dad. However, there are many other things you could offer in whatever you specialize in.

4. You could become a professional hunting guide. I was watching a show about guides in Alaska, who take hunters on extremely remote hunts. I can't imagine the money they pull in for multi-day hunts. It doesn't only apply to the remote places either. You could easily do a job like this in a town like where lived. Let me say one more time, this is all legit guided hunting trips. I'm not talking about anything illegal.

Again, when we grow up doing something day in and day out, we have a tendency to take it for granted and have an extremely closed mind for the opportunities around us. You see, I grew up with land galore along with the opportunity to hunt at any given moment. It didn't intrigue me, and I never took advantage of it. If you will take a moment and look around and search for the opportunity with what you already have, the possibilities are absolutely limitless.

To drive this point home, my sister, who lives in Florida, was talking to some guys who were about to embark on a deer hunting trip. These were men who didn't have land in their backyard, nor an entire herd of deer to watch from their back porch every night, like we had. They were getting ready to fly out and spend $2500 each on the chance to shoot a deer - one deer. I admit I was shocked that someone was willing to pay that. An opportunity I had in childhood and didn't think twice about, nor even cared about, was something someone was willing to drop $2500 to experience just once!

5. You could create a YouTube channel (before you shut me down on this one, think for a moment of those Disney people). You could review products via video, give hunting advice, or you could take people on hunts and record the outing. You could then make money from the ads they play while people watch. Or who knows, you could get picked up as a host for a hunting show. Don't laugh. Some people are hosts on television today because they became YouTube famous first

One more thing about YouTube and advertising. You never know what people will be looking for with video. I never dreamed I would search for a video of 'Cows Mooing.' Yes, I searched for that when my son was one and obsessed with farm animals. We watched those videos over and over. It made me appreciate the time people took to put up a video on what they probably took for granted every day. You just never know!

6. We could also do the standard brick and motor and/or online store, and you could create a store that sells hunting supplies. If you want to get crazy, look at places like Cabela's and Bass Pro to see what they are missing. What could you do differently, or what are some other things you could offer? Could you offer more personalized customer service or more specialized products? You could take this one hobby and make something as big or as small as you want to out of it.

7. Here is a bonus. Finally, you could create books or online tutorials about how to get started in hunting or tips and tricks for being more successful. You could conduct interviews with other successful hunters, and tell the stories about what makes them more successful. You could teach others how to create their own business around hunting.

8. Another idea is to create an online community of hunters. Charge them a monthly fee to be a part of it, and match up hunters to guides. Offer a place where they can ask questions, etc.

I could list way more. Honestly, I can't say this enough. We are in a day and age where you are not limited by where you grew up, or what you know, or what education you have. You can find out anything and everything you could ever want, and make money teaching it to others.

It doesn't matter if your hobby is extremely basic. If you really want to create a living doing it, and you put some thought and work behind it, you could make money. Excuses don't matter because I'm sure someone out there had far worse odds, and they're standing on the other side, triumphant and successful.

If you want more ideas on businesses you could start, get my free list with over 50 ideas at: http://thestartersclub.com/50_businesses

I hope I have made this clear. It genuinely is all yours for the taking. Remember this excellent advice: if you're great at something, no matter what it is, it becomes your duty to share it with the world by teaching others. So you can either make excuses about why you can't, or you can move forward believing that you can.

Either way, you're going to be right.

Business models can be a thing that trip up a lot of people. First, let me cover what a business model is. To put it simply, a business model is the plan of how you're going to make money. It will determine what product or service you will provide, and how you will make money from it. The definition from Google.com is: *'a design for the successful operation of a business, identifying revenue sources, customer base, products, and details of financing.'*

When you get this idea for a business, there are a few questions you have to ask yourself. First, it is not just about a product or service you sell to make money. You have to factor in the costs to make it, how you're going to produce it, and how you're going to market it. Then you have to figure out who exactly is going to want to buy this product. The third step is figuring out how you're going to finance the costs that will be required to get this business not only off the ground, but also building.

For example, the YouTube channel from the beginning of this chapter has a simple business model. They put out content (opening Disney product boxes), build subscribers (parents of toddlers), and then make money from the advertising. (Basically, they get paid for allowing ads to show up on their videos.)

If you work in the corporate world, making money is relatively straightforward. You work and every few weeks a paycheck shows up in your bank account. Whether you work per hour, on commission, salary, or a combination, the premise is simple. You trade time for money.

In the entrepreneur world, the concept can be just as basic, again trading time for money. Either you create a service and get paid for completing that service, such as consulting or performing a job like cleaning gutters, or proofreading résumés. There is no fixed list of services in the world. You do have to tie a value to your service, and if someone is willing to pay for it, you have a business.

The other side of business models in the entrepreneur world comes through products. Before I immersed myself in this world, the only I way I thought you could do this was by inventing a new product to sell. You could invent a product, make sure it is patented and protected, and then find someone to either sell the product for you (known as wholesale), or sell it directly from your own store or website.

Both of these business models are very fundamental, and as simple as they are, putting them to work can be quite daunting. When it comes to services, you have to know what you're doing. The harder part can be believing you are actually worth the price you're going to ask someone to pay.

As for the product side, you would have to think of a new product and put it all together. You may have to create the mold and find someone to manufacture it. Then you have to find ways to have it produced where you can make money selling it. Don't forget selling points and marketing, which can be hard tasks for someone who has never done it before. You would either have to come up with money to hire someone to help you, or do it all yourself.

As easy or as difficult as these two options may look to you, there is a lot of gray in the middle that will help you figure out how to create a business.

Let's look into that gray matter on services side first. There is consulting, where you're an expert in something. You can teach others what you know, or put your expertise to work to help them with their life or business. You can charge for these services per hour or per job.

This can be a good and a bad thing. If you ever read 'Rich Dad, Poor Dad' by Robert Kiyosaki, this is the Self-Employed Quadrant. Yes, you are working for yourself, which is great. However, the money you make depends on how many hours you are putting in. The problem with this is that you don't make money while you sleep, or while you go on vacation. So if you do decide to take on a business like this, I would encourage you to find a way to make it scalable. You want to have either others working for you, or products in addition to your services, so the money you make no longer is dependent on the time you put in. You can build your clientele, and hire other people who know what you do (or teach them to know what you know), and then they can help do more consulting.

Another thing you can do to make money is to create online courses. This is a booming industry, and according to Forbes, is set to do over $107 billion dollars in 2015[1].

An online course is exactly how it sounds. You put together content, and can teach others online who would like to learn that. Either you can record video of you walking through certain items via PowerPoint, or screen capturing yourself doing the work. You can also record yourself teaching the content.

---

[1] http://www.forbes.com/sites/tjmccue/2014/08/27/online-learning-industry-poised-for-107-billion-in-2015/

Courses do blur the lines between services and products. Basically, you are turning your service into a product that can be sold time and time again. The same blur applies to books. Suddenly the product side isn't as black and white as inventing a product, creating molds, finding manufacturers, etc. You're ultimately creating the product (this also can include books too) and selling them as an extension to your services.

Let's return to the basic services example. For my pet sitting company, I was paid per job. I then hired people, and paid them a portion of what I received. I could have taken that to another level, and added other services such as dog grooming or dog training. I then could have blurred the lines between service and products with the addition of teaching other people how to start their own pet sitting companies. I could have created contracts and policies and procedures and sold the templates to other people.

Do you see the gray area? Having a service doesn't mean that is all you have to do because products can always easily be added.

Now let's go to the products side. By selling someone else's products, you can blur the line of services. You don't necessarily have to be the product creator. You can find other's products at wholesale, and then sell them either via a website or storefront. You might be freaked out by the upfront cost required to buy all of the inventory to sell, but there is a workaround for that too. I was introduced to drop shipping several years ago for another business I was helping to build.

In drop shipping, you may list a product on a website, but you never have to actually stock the item. You can find a wholesaler who will drop ship the item for you. So every time anyone orders the product from your website, you collect the money, send a request to the wholesaler, and they send the product out to the buyer for you. Instead of worrying about inventory, you are simply paying for the product per sale.

When I say you can create a business truly out of anything, I'm not lying. Let's stick with animals. As an animal lover, you decide you would love to sell cute dog clothes. Instead of a ton of upfront costs, all you need is a registered business, a website, a way to track inventory, and a few wholesale contacts that carry the items you love. You put the products on your website, and collect the money for the purchase. Then you just send a notification to the drop shipper (the company holding the product) to send that item to the address of your customer.

Let me delve even more into services and products. If you are wondering what in the world you could consult in because, well, maybe you haven't done anything you feel is remarkable, there is still a lot you could teach others. Let me first remind you that knowing EVERYTHING about a particular subject isn't required before you can label yourself an expert. It is merely knowing more about a subject than someone else.

Let's say you want to start a business where you're doing consulting, and to start scaling your business you could hire employees to take on some of the work. Hiring them will allow you to bring on more customers. Now, let's say you want to add an additional revenue stream and you can help people who can't quite afford to hire you or your employees. Let's say your consulting business helps people with marketing their business. You could create an online course that teaches the basics of setting up a marketing campaign for a business. You can get paid each time someone buys that course. You could also create a paid membership site, where you offer more value about marketing, a community of other business owners also trying to build their business, and possibly monthly tutorials where you get more in-depth around a specific topic.

Your business model is now this: making money on your services, employee services, courses you sell, plus the monthly membership. Your business model is no longer black and white (performing a service, trading time for money), but now it has all kinds of shades of gray.

You don't have to have an elaborate business model like this all figured out at the beginning. When you are starting out, it's simple; you just need to figure out what one thing you will sell. You then need to know who you are going to sell it too, what it will cost to begin and run, and how you will get the money to put the business together.

Just like anything in life, as you move forward, your business will evolve. However, you just have to begin in order to see how that happens and what opportunities arise.

Chapter 5

Define Your Why(s)!

Let's talk about your 'why'. Hopefully, you've started thinking about what it is that makes you tick. You have realized a passion, something you may want to make a life around. Now it's time to understand what your 'why' really is. I believe this is one of the most crucial pieces to your business success.

The concept of the 'why' was brought up by Simon Sineck several years ago. He wrote a book called 'It Starts With Why', and had a very popular Ted Talk [2] that covers the topic. It is all about understanding what made certain companies great. It wasn't because they sold a great product or offered a great service. It was because they had an amazing 'why' driving the reason for their entire business. People just didn't buy a product; they aligned with a movement because the business was so clear about why they did what they did.

2

http://www.ted.com/talks/simon_sinek_how_great_leaders_inspire_action?language=en

An example from his talk where he specifically references Apple: *'Apple's message is not 'we make great computers. They're beautifully designed, simple to use and user-friendly. Want to buy one?' Here's how Apple actually communicates: 'everything we do, we believe in challenging the status quo. We believe in thinking differently. The way we challenge the status quo is by making our products beautifully designed, simple to use, and user-friendly. We just happen to make great computers. Want to buy one?'*

To me, the message was profound. Your 'why' will determine everything. It will determine what gets you up in the morning to continue building this business. It will also help build a community and inspire people to be part of what you're offering.

I believe in your business there needs to be two sides to your 'why'. First, there has to be a personal side, and it has to be more than just wanting to make lots of money. When I ask my clients what their 'why' is, the typical answer is: 'I want to live a passion' or 'I want to build a legacy for my children.' Both of which are great answers to drive you. However, that is it. They're driving YOU. Yes, building a legacy is great, but will someone buy one of your products or services because they too love your children? Probably not.

Your other 'why' has to be what your company is about, not what you do or how you do it, but WHY you do it. Too many people don't give this enough thought, and it can make or break your business. I was lucky in my first two businesses. I happened upon two great 'whys', and it made hiring people easy and finding clients I loved even easier.

I didn't build my first business to become rich. I had no idea it would lead me to money. I simply wanted to provide people with a no stress option to leaving their home that I couldn't find for myself. I loved animals, and I loved knowing people could enjoy their vacation. I was diligent about only hiring people who shared my values, which made it easy for me to expand.

My second business' 'why' was driven from the fact that at my mom had skin cancer, and my skin told the story that I was on the same path. I wanted an option for people that made them feel beautiful and natural without having to succumb their skin to the sun. My 'why' wasn't to make money; it was to make people healthier while still feeling beautiful.

Starting a business isn't just about making lots of money. Your personal 'why' should be a force so large, that no matter what goes wrong, no matter how hard your day is, your 'why' is going to carry you through it. Your business 'why' should be something that people can't wait to represent, to stand behind, and to be a part of. It should give a reason for why your company does what it does that represents more than a bottom line.

Take an extra moment to re-read that paragraph. The rest of this chapter is going to attempt to underscore just what that means.

Once you identify what your passion is and what makes you tick, the next step is grasping your whys. Doing so will drive home the enthusiasm for your business.

Understand there may come a point in your business where the excitement fades. You may find yourself in a position where you have worked hard, but people aren't flocking in like you thought they would. You may feel like you want to give up and quit, but you can't! I want you to understand this is the norm. These are the expectations you should have, and if you keep moving forward, things will change. You don't give up. You simply get through that point, and I promise if your personal 'why' is strong enough, it will get you through the hard moments in your business.

I know I say this frequently; but by no means do I say it to discourage you. I want you to know the truth so when things are hard, you understand that it's not you who is the problem. Hard things just happen. Know that there isn't an entrepreneur who doesn't go through this. Your 'why' will get you through those hard times. When you're ready to jump on Monster.com to look for that next job, your 'why' will make you stop.

I'll use my fiancé as another example. If he could single handedly make the world a healthier place he would. He is a chiropractor but specializes in the cases that no one can seem to fix, and he has spent countless hours mastering Applied Kinesiology. He even loves his profession so much that he teaches AK to students across the nation because he sees it as a way to reach more people.

This is a driving force for him, and honestly I'm not sure what he would do if he couldn't have his practice. But oh yes, he has to run a business in order to live this purpose and mission. Entrepreneurship hasn't been easy for him, and there have been some rough times. However, this passion for what he does is what drives him. Even when he's having a hard day, all it takes is one moment for him, where he literally changes someone's life and the bad stuff doesn't matter.

Many will never feel that passion towards anything that makes us money, and it is a shame.

If you discover your true passion and find a need, then begin building that business. If this business adds value to the world, and you work hard at it, I promise you, something will come from it. I can't promise you will make millions, but I also understand that making millions isn't everyone's goals. I just promise you with a strong idea, strong research, a strong desire, this can potentially become something.

Let's break down exactly what a 'why' is so you can start putting yours together. Your personal 'why' is a combination of three things.

First, it's something that makes you come alive.

We've talked a lot about your passion so far. Your passion is obviously very important in the cultivation of your 'why'. It has to be something that makes you happy. If you had two hours a week of spare time, and where money meant nothing, what exactly would you do?

The answer to that question should explain a lot about your passion. Would you read books about a certain topic? Would you want to learn something new? If you had just an extra hour in the day to do anything, what would interest you?

Second, it's where your innate strengths lie.

This is a big one. We are all given gifts. Not everyone shares the same gifts. To not cultivate those gifts, those innate strengths, and share them with the world, is doing a disservice to it. Not to mention that not cultivating those does a huge disservice to yourself.

We are all here to do something. There are things that come so easy to each one of us, that we have no idea that they are gifts. We have naturally been able to do them all of our lives, so we don't think twice about them. For example, I love to speak. I love to meet people. I discovered a huge strength of mine is getting on a stage and sharing my message. I love it! It makes me feel alive when I step on that stage, and nothing brings me greater joy when someone tells me how I've helped to push them to a new level.

I could have merely thought that sure, I do like to get up in front of people and speak, but I wasn't going to do it. I could have thought that since it came so easy to me, that everyone must love to get up on stage and speak. Yes, that is an extreme example because so many people are terrified of public speaking, but you see my point. Instead of just pushing this aside and thinking it is easy for everyone, I made the conscious decision to use that gift along with my story and share it with the world.

It's not conceited to believe by sharing your gift, you're making the world a better place. I know many people might get hung up on that. Recognize that telling your story and using your gifts, can give someone else enough courage to do exactly what you're doing: Following your passion!

Third, part of your personal 'why' is how you want your life to be measured.

As you are thinking about how you want to live your life and use your business to help others, consider one thing. Think about what is going to be important to you when you sit back and ask yourself if you gave it your all. If working the corporate job, and raising your kids, and retiring is enough for you, then becoming an entrepreneur probably won't be on your radar. If you have an idea and know if you don't follow through with it, you will have regrets, it is probably time to get moving.

Dig deep into these three facets, define them, and you can cultivate your 'why'. I am very serious about how important your 'why' is. It will make you keep going. It gives you an end goal. It's going to constantly remind you of why you need to continue doing what you're doing, and it's going to push you out of your comfort zones. When we have a 'why' so great and so strong within us, we can't sit around and ignore it. If you truly let yourself feel it, there will be nothing to will stop you from pursuing it.

Your 'why' will drive you, and it will eat your core alive until you have no choice but to get up, move forward, and start living it.

Are there bad personal whys? Of course. One off the top of my head would be you hate your boss. Although this is a great reason to move out of a comfort zone, you can always find a better boss. Even with a better boss, though, you will still be doing what you may not like. I had it happen to me. I left a job because I hated my boss - beyond belief - but I managed to find the same job with a boss I loved. So if you can simply go out and find a better boss, there is no real motivation to push you when times get tough.

Another bad 'why' is because you merely want to try something different. You can't just want to *try* a thing. As the great Yoda said, and it's one of my favorite quotes to this day, *'You either do or do not; there is no try.'* To me, the word 'try' is frankly a cop out. It gives us permission to not go all in. It gives us permission to give up whenever we want. I hate it when I have an event or a get-together, and someone tells me they will try to make it. I can pretty much guarantee they're not going to be there.

A 'why' is also not because you think you might like something. No, a 'why' should equate to a fire and passion. As I mentioned, it has to be something so strong, if you don't do it, you are wounding yourself. A personal 'why' has to - and I mean HAS to - equate to passion, hunger, craving, and desire. And that's the truth of it. It can't be because you think you might perhaps maybe like something. You have to know with everything you have. It's a must.

Liking just won't cut it. You have to LOVE it and be 100% passionate for it.

Let me explain it to you this way. If you're a woman and have already had a child, you can fully relate to this. There is nothing, not one thing that was easy about labor. (And if you try to tell me there was, I will hurt you!). Labor was hard. Probably THE hardest thing you have ever done. Even those last two months of pregnancy were hard. Now looking back at how hard it was, and how there were no easy moments, you can easily say it was one of the best things that ever happened to you.

If you aren't a two-legged parent, there is no shame in bringing up the four-legged example. If you have ever dealt with a puppy, once again, I can say there wasn't a whole lot that was easy about it. There was a lot of work. You had to watch that puppy like a hawk to potty train, and some of you may have had a few sleepless nights.

However, now you can look over at the full-grown dog and love them more than you ever could have imagined. It was hard, but it was well worth it. And that's what I want to drive home about entrepreneurship. You have to be in it, to really be in it. I've seen too many people take that naughty puppy back to the shelter, and they never get to experience the good stuff. The calm dog who is concerned about you when you're sad, who watches out for your safety, and is an ever loving companion. They never get to experience the great moments when that dog truly does become your best friend.

Yes, these are two extreme examples, but my point is that something made you push through the hard stuff. You wanted something so badly, that no matter how hard it was, you didn't stop. You didn't think that yeah maybe you should try this baby stuff, and then when month five of the pregnancy came along you decided it wasn't worth it. You pushed through. You had a massive why driving you. The same thing should be applied to your business.

Another 'why' you should not have is that you want to make money. Listen, if you're in need of money immediately, then entrepreneurship is a path that you shouldn't be taking. It always seems to cost a little more and take a little longer than you originally thought. So if you are looking for a quick fix in the money world, then I would advise that you stick with your corporate job because that is going to pay you faster than your own business will.

Let me give you an example of my two personal 'whys', and what drives me every day in my business. Maybe it will give you a few ideas when creating your own.

My first is my kids. Now I understand this is very typical, and everyone wants a better life for their kids. But it's not the better life that's my driving reason. Like I mentioned earlier, there's a quote that states: '*Your children will grow to be who you are, so be who you want them be.*' I read this quote shortly after I had my first son, and it forever changed my life.

You see, I spent a very long time, standing on the edge, completely terrified to take a chance on myself. If you read 'Rich

69

Dad, Poor Dad,' my dad was of the poor dad mentality (although he was an entrepreneur himself). He felt that I should get a job and be safe. I had built businesses of my own but was always scared to take that final leap (leaving Corporate America).

It wasn't until I had children and read that quote when I realized my kids were going to look at me as an example. If I wanted them to not live in fear, then I had to jump into my fears with both feet and move forward. I had to do this not only for myself but my kids.

As I move forward in my business, this rings truer than ever. Now that I have leaped through my fears, and I'm pushing forward, resistance is naturally bound to happen. I can do one of two things. I can go back to work, and say it's just easier. Or I can keep pushing through, and be the example that quitting is not an option. It's a 'why' I absolutely can't ignore. I could never live with myself if I didn't follow through. I have to be the example that I have promised myself I would be for my kids.

My second 'why' is another giant raging point that I have to do to know I've fulfilled what it is I need to do for my time on earth. If you know me for any given period, you'll learn I'm a huge animal lover. Like so much I have six freaking dogs. I have no desire to have six dogs, and although I love every single one very much, having a few less does sound refreshing at times.

However, this is a passion of mine. I can be exhausted, done with animals, and then the moment I walk into a shelter, I melt. As long as there are dogs dying in shelters every day, I will forever be an advocate of saving them. It can be hard, but it brings me one of the greatest joys in my life.

So with that, a dream of mine has always been to own a Rottweiler rescue. I've worked with rescues, and I see how they operate, and they can be grueling. Money is hard to come by, and you are constantly running fund-raisers and such, to try to get dog food to your fosters, medical expenses paid, etc. It feels like you can either have a full-time job or a rescue, but you can't have both.

My 'why' is to personally change that. If I died tomorrow without ever starting my rescue, my time here on earth would not have been fulfilled. Yes, you're right, that sounds crazy harsh, but it's the truth. I want my company to be able to fund the rescue, and I'm not tied to fundraisers for the next needed surgery to happen. I want to be able to help as many dogs as I can help. Working my corporate job was not going to get me there.

So for me, when the going gets tough, I have two choices. I can go back and never live my true purpose, or I can push ahead and make the difference I've always dreamed of making in this world.

I have a great story about why having a 'why' is so important. Just a few days ago, I hit a wall. A wall so hard, I was lying in bed and told my fiancé I wanted to quit. I know I would never have actually quit, but I was tempted. The day earlier I had spent several hours spinning on something that *should* have taken me twenty minutes (welcome to entrepreneurship). I was mad at myself for wasting that time, when I could have spent with my kids.

I was having some serious struggles with the whole motherhood and working mom balance, and I wondered if I was a terrible mother by working on my dreams, too.

I woke up the next morning still feeling crappy, and in the middle of work, I took a quick Facebook break. What I found on my page left me in tears for literally thirty minutes. A friend of mine had posted a story about a Rottie that was rescued and was underweight and almost hairless due to mange. They showed the before and after pictures, and in the after, he was healthy but just as importantly, he was also happy.

This is exactly one of the reasons I do what I do. To have that moment laid right out for me - that quitting wasn't an option - left me pretty emotional. Honestly, that is why you have a 'why' that drives you. So when moments like that strike, quitting isn't an item on your list of possibilities. Pushing through and figuring it out are the only two things you can do.

Is it starting to make more sense about how strong this needs to be?

Let's cover a little bit about the business 'why'. I think this is equally as important as your personal one because this is going to help your customers align with your message. It is also going to be something that your employees, or even people who contract for you, can get excited about.

I look at your business 'why' as where you feel you add value to the world. Your product or service just happens to be the 'thing' that gets you there.

Your 'why' can be tied to your strengths. However, we all have something that we want to do to change the world.

Understand that believing you can make a difference is enough, and having that desire can drive so much in your business. It will get people excited about what you do, and excited to join what you are creating.

For me, I linked my strength of being able to break down things in a very simplistic approach to wanting to help as many people as I could to change their lives.

My business 'why' is simple: To inspire others to live a life of their dreams by opening their eyes to opportunities. Then we make those opportunities possible by teaching no bull business basics.

A business 'why' does sound very similar to a mission statement. However, a mission statement is slightly different. It typically consists of three things which are you key market, your contribution, and your distinction.

Digging deep and defining your 'whys' will help to make a major difference in your business.

It is seriously all that simple. Those are my whys that keep me going on a daily basis. When I may lose momentum or hit a stumbling block, I know with push and persistence, better things are on the horizon. And my personal 'whys' are what carry me.

Search for your 'why'. Define a strong enough 'why', and there should be nothing that stops you. Let's say your dream is own a bakery. You've never even worked in a bakery before, but that shouldn't be the reason that stops you. Even if you're working a full-time day job, you should want this so badly you will figure out how to learn the process.

You can work for one, learn about it, or see if you can help out a couple of nights a week. You can tell them your plan, volunteer a couple of mornings a week to help out, and watch what happens. Find out what this is all about. Just like I talked about in Chapter 2, you may not love it. However, if it's truly a passion, it will only ignite the fire within you to keep going and want it more than you could have ever imagined.

You can take it a step further and read up on it. Buy some books. Start something small out of your own home. (Amazon was started out of Jeff Bezos' garage). You can do anything and everything you put your mind to. But you do have to actually do it. You have to put one foot in front of the other. And you have to have a 'why' pushing you so hard, that there's just no possibility for you to go back.

With a strong enough personal and business 'why' and with a passion, you can truly do anything you set your mind to. If you're reading this and coming up with some excuse as to why you can't, then I'm going to call you out on it. It's an excuse, and you don't want it bad enough because let me say that again: with a strong enough 'why', and passion, you can do ANYTHING. Sit down and figure out why you want this, and then make a plan to get it.

I look back at so many moments of my life when I wasn't sure I could get through. The example of picking up and moving to Phoenix is one of them. It was one of the hardest things I ever could have done; yet it was worth every single hard moment that I endured. I learned so much about myself, so much about what it takes actually to take a chance, and it's a life lesson fifteen years later I share with you because it forever changed my life.

That's why there is a foundation to the start and why I've written this book. That's why I want your foundation of starting so solid that there is nothing that can hold you back. This is why I want you to understand your personal 'why', so there is absolutely nothing to stop you.

Yes, if being an entrepreneur were easy, then everyone would do it. You won't make millions of dollars in a week from building a website. You won't launch your first product and make hundreds of thousands of dollars. It takes work. It actually takes a lot of work. It's a quest that will forever change your life, but again, has anything life changing ever been easy?

It's going to take guts. It's going to take hustle. It's going to take everything you have, and then digging to find some more. Think of your 'whys' as specially designed shovels there to let you dig as deeply as you need to go.

Chapter 6

Redefine Your Beliefs

All of this owning your own business thing is not too good to be true. It is possible, and I've met many, many people who are making lots of money doing it. Once again, it's not because they're crazy special or super smart. It's not because they're better at it than you. It is simply because they never gave up. They had an idea, did something about it, maybe made a mistake or two but kept at it. When it all came down to it, they hustled their asses off.

I had this conversation with a friend of mine the other day who was trying to help out a stay-at-home mom going through a divorce. This mom been home for several years and didn't have a good idea about how to get back into the corporate world. My friend suggested she start training herself online on various programs and tools. From there she could begin doing some work as a Virtual Assistant. If she learned the right skills, she could still work from home, make her own schedule, and charge up to $60 an hour for her time. (Which is true.)

The woman shut down the idea, immediately. Instead of thinking this was also a great idea, instead of considering the possibilities and the endless options for her, instead of researching how she could break into this new profession, her reasoning was this: It sounded too good to be true.

Granted my friend wasn't trying to sell some get rich quick scheme. She told her there would be work involved. She told her in order to be successful, she would have to specialize and learn different things on her own. And yes, she would have to market herself, too. There was no promise of random people just begging her to take their money in exchange for helping them.

But the answer was still, 'it's too good to be true.' She believed this because her life was limited by only the things she felt to be true versus other things that had the possibility to become true.

I tell you this because you have one of two outcomes from reading this book. You can think I'm crazy, and that I don't know what I'm talking about. You can also think everything I'm putting in front of you is too good to be true.

The other option is you could say to yourself, 'you know what, I want this bad enough. Plus my 'why' is strong enough, and I'm going to do this.' (Notice my words were not: 'I'm going to give this a try.' There is no trying. Either you're all in or you're not.)

As I said, I'm not telling you that you're going to make millions tomorrow. I'm simply telling you that life is yours for the writing. If it's millions you want, with the right vision, the right product or service, and the right work ethic, millions are very possible. If it's just an extra thousand dollars a month so you can supplement your family without getting another part time job, then by all means, it is still possible.

Do not limit yourself by what you learned while growing up. Don't limit yourself to only the things you only believe to be true for whatever reason. Don't limit yourself. Start dreaming. Start thinking 'bigger picture,' and all of these things are possible.

One of the most profound moments for me happened last year when I met my friend Danette. Growing up on a farm, I worked hard for money. By no means was anything we had easy. Even as I worked the corporate job, I still worked really hard outside of it to make the great money. My belief was that money was possible, but it wasn't easy to come by.

I remember when Danette, made the statement 'money is easy to make.' I was shocked. I was thirty-seven years old, and never in my life had ever heard anyone say that. Money was EASY to make? I sat on it for a long time, and realized that because of the way I grew up I had this belief ingrained in me that money was hard to come by. I had no idea I could actually change this and create the reality that it was easy to make.

Here's another perfect example. Marie Forleo is someone I found online. It was at just the right moment when she was selling the exact thing I needed at the time I found her. Marie does marketing all year round, but then releases her signature online program - B-School

- once a year. I happened upon her just as she was releasing her 2013 course.

Please know these are not exact numbers, and I'm simply going off memory. But I want to say in 2013, around 4,000 people were added to her private community, which was only accessible by purchasing the program. At a price of $1997, that's over $7,000,000. Not bad pocket change. Now the next year, it was about 7,000 people added to the group. You can do the math and see that wouldn't be bad money to make once a year. Granted, I'm not going to get technical and talk about her business costs, etc. That is not the point. Even if you could make $1,000,000 from a launch every year, I would bet that it's more than you are making in your corporate job.

Now, let me just say that unless you're insanely lucky, you're not going to sell 4,000 units of your online course or program for $1997 the first time you go live. However, even if you charged $997 and sold five, that's not bad money starting out. I know many Americans could use that to help pay the bills. Then imagine you keep working, you get a great reputation, you start building an amazing community, and you can sell more. Maybe you double and add ten more people the next time. You could then double again and add twenty. From there you start getting so popular, that you decide to add a bit more value and double the price. The zeros start tacking on quickly, and suddenly you're making way more than you ever did in your corporate life.

So the answer to the question 'is it all too good to be true?' is definitely 'NO.' The question should be, 'is it possible?' And to that, the answer is 'YES.' You just have to keep at it, keep moving, keep taking steps forward, and you'll start seeing the 'too good to be true' results. You're just probably not going to see them the moment you start your business.

I also want you to nix the belief that everything has to be perfect. One of my favorite sayings is 'perfect is the enemy of done.'

I'm going to talk in another chapter about self-sabotage getting the best of you when we start thinking of perfection. However, there's also this worry we will put something out there, and someone will find the flaws in it.

Let me be honest, putting yourself out there is really scary, and there is just no easier way to say it. When you start to grow, people will come out, complete strangers even, to put you down. Haters are going to hate, and let me just say, if you're a hater, and you're reading this, for goodness sakes, can you please stop? Your jealousy does no one any good. If you truly feel the need to do something, then please just take that time and effort and do it into making yourself better instead of putting everyone else down. Just stop!! I never get the people who follow people they don't like, only to put them down later. It just never made any sense to me.

I digress, though. Let me get back to the fact that putting yourself out there will attract haters. This does nothing to help our fear of success. With success comes criticism, and with criticism comes feeling like crap. I experienced this first hand with my fiancé. I finally, after begging and pleading for years, convinced him to share his knowledge via a blog. It took so much encouraging and cajoling that when I finally got him to start writing, I was beyond thrilled.

Once he got in his writing groove, there seemed to be no stopping him. Ideas flowed, and I actually had to tell him to slow down. He was so excited about it that he kept going and going. Unfortunately, it all changed pretty quickly when the first critics showed up.

I had become bold and started putting his content on Reddit. Even though this one article had gone through three different editors, the word that should have been 'flour' was written as 'flower.' It was a simple mistake, and yes, it should have been caught. But the fact was, it wasn't.

Several people picked up on it, of course, and made comments about a person who would write 'flower' instead of 'flour.' I saw it crush him. He went from publishing several articles at a time to barely getting one out a week. Instead of saying what was bothering him, he used SEO as a cop out. His articles weren't optimized enough, and therefore he couldn't publish them until they were.

But I know it was that single crushing moment where he had put himself out there, made a mistake, and was called on it. He went from being on fire, to feeling like he shouldn't be blogging at all.

I spent MONTHS – AGAIN - convincing him that he needed to pick it back up. People would get valuable information from his blog posts. I told him he couldn't let a few people bring him down. If nothing was out there, no matter how SEO optimized it was, no one would ever find it. Finally, he picked it up again, but it was a valuable lesson for both of us.

Here are a few things you should realize when it comes time to believing in yourself.

First, mistakes are going to happen, and it is just the nature of the beast. Put your head down, and do the best you can do. If you need to hire others to help, I would encourage it. However, please don't feel that perfect is the only way to get your product or service to the world. If someone finds a mistake, acknowledge it, and fix it. I promise you two days later they probably won't even remember it!

To hit this one home, a great quote by Ried Hoffman, the founder of LinkedIn, is: *'If you are not embarrassed by the first version of your product, you've launched too late.'* You will make mistakes, and that's simply the name of the game. However, customers will never find you if you have nothing out there to show. Everyone starts somewhere, and that is 100% fact.

Second, there are going to be people who don't like your product or service, or don't like you, and they're going to tell you no. Guess what? THAT'S OKAY! It really is okay. I was ecstatic the first time someone made a mean comment to me. It meant I had gotten out to more people than just my friends and family. It also meant I was posting stuff that wasn't meant for everyone to like. I always give this advice to brides to be: *'you will never make everyone happy so just do what will make YOU happy.'*

The same advice can be given to entrepreneurs, just with a bit of added twist. *'You will never make everyone happy, so just be YOU.'* Be yourself. You don't have to go out and bash people who don't believe in what you do. Just worry about you and the message you want to give to the world, and the good stuff will follow.

The third thing you need to consider is that NOT copying anyone else will get you further much faster in whatever you are doing. This one can be tough because if someone else is doing it right, we feel the need to do it like they do. Being yourself, and 100% yourself, may not resonate with someone. But it *will* resonate well with the people whom you intend (or 'the people you have in mind'). I will get into this more in another chapter.

Fourth, there are going to be hard times, and you have to push through knowing this is what you're supposed to be doing. As I mentioned, this is why your 'why' is so important.

Through those hard times, you have to believe in yourself. You have to be driven. You have to know that going back is not possible. This happened when I finally quit my job. Now that I have finally left that soul-sucking job behind and lived this life, 'the good life,' I don't believe I could ever go back.

Yes, there are moments that are scary. Still! You have to listen to what's driving you and pushing you, and I promise when you start that journey forward, going back will seem impossible.

There is not one entrepreneur in the world who had all the answers before they started out. They didn't know everything. They just knew they had a dream, and a burning desire so intense they couldn't NOT follow it.

I remember hearing the story of The Daily Love, which was created by Maston Kipp. He was almost out of money, and living in someone's guesthouse. He was thinking it might be time to give up on his dream, even though he knew what he was doing had the potential to be amazing. Just when he doubted himself the most, one retweet from Kim Kardashian telling her audience how awesome he was, changed everything overnight.[3]

Daymond John, the owner of Fubu, was turned down by over twenty private investors. His mom convinced him to put an ad in the paper. It was there where Samsung found it and became an investor in his company and took him to the next level.[4]

Howard Shultz, the CEO of Starbucks, was initially turned down by the original owners of Starbucks (who just sold coffee beans at the time) when he told them his vision for Italian type coffee shops. He spoke to 242 investors, and 217 of them told him no[5]. They told him the idea was crazy, and that no one in the United States would pay more than $1.50 for a cup of coffee. But he kept pushing because he

---

[3] http://www.huffingtonpost.com/2013/08/28/mastin-kipp-daily-love-kim-kardashian_n_3830746.html
[4] http://daymondjohn.com/about/
[5] http://www.entrepreneur.com/article/15582

truly believed in his concept. Now the thought of life without Starbucks makes me shudder!

I could tell story after story after story about entrepreneurs who had people telling them what they were doing wasn't right, or that they weren't going to make it. I'm sure every single one of them at some point started to believe it. However, it was that burning desire and belief that became so strong, they couldn't *not* go through with it.

That is why you have to have more than just a desire to start a business. You have to have a strong 'why' and follow it. You may start telling yourself that you're crazy, or you're stupid, but you have to shush that inner voice. You can't tell yourself you don't know what you're doing. You have to start putting one foot in front of the other and move. Answers that you don't have will begin to appear, I promise you.

You have to change your beliefs that all of this is possible, even if people don't like you or turn you down.

Being an entrepreneur is really about two main things.

1. The willingness to learn what you don't know and to ask the questions to get those answers.
2. The willingness to understand what you don't know, and hire people who are smarter than you.

The first one is easier. You have to realize that Google is truly your best friend, and between books and Google, you can pretty much learn anything you can ever imagined.

You've got this. It is possible. Get those doubts out of your mind. You will run into roadblocks, and you're going to have to back up and go a different route, and that's okay. The point is that you don't listen to the haters (even if it's a voice in your head that's doing the hating). But that instead you be yourself, be 100% true to you and keep your business going in a forward motion.

Believe this is possible, and you will soon discover that it is!

Chapter 7

Prepare for Self Sabotage

I'm not kidding when I say this, and I mean prepare yourself because it is coming. You are about to embark on something big. You are about to begin something that excites you. You are about to finally do this thing that you had always had in the back of your mind that you would like to do. However, you have spent far too much time talking yourself out of it. This is something that you align with, and you are about to finally take that first step to make it happen.

However, the inner thoughts, which you may not even be aware you are thinking, will begin to creep in. What happens if you finally do this, go all in, but you fail? What happens if you go all in, and you succeed? Are you possibly scared that something bad might happen if you get everything you have ever wanted?

Many people laugh at the idea of the fear of success. How could anyone possibly be afraid of success? After all, this is what you have always wanted. To think that there is the possibility of any self-sabotaging going on is just absolutely crazy.

Yet, it happens all the time.

- Have you ever seen a frivolous lawsuit mentioned in the news, and thought you would never want to put yourself in that situation?

- Have you ever thought about hiring someone, and then wondered what would happen if they couldn't portray the same vision as you? Or have you worried that hiring someone might screw up the entire thing?

- Have you ever wondered what if you get your business to a certain level where you're able to sell it, but then someone else takes over making the decisions, and your baby is not yours anymore?

- Have you over emphasized that one thing you have hinged all of your happiness on that you begin to wonder if you can do it? A great example of this is the person who will be happy when, let's say they lose 10 pounds. They know that all the happiness they ever wanted is hinging on just 10 pounds. So why do they never make those steps to make it happen?

  - Do you get stressed out thinking about the possible pressure you may feel when you have hit that higher level?

If you have answered 'yes' to any of these things, then you can see that having a fear of success isn't so silly.

What happens when you do have it all? Will it be as awesome as you thought it would feel? Will people come out of the woodwork to try to take what you have worked so hard for? Will it be all that you thought it was?

It is these limiting thoughts, whether you think them out loud or not, that hold you back. You may not work quite as hard on something. You may find just one more thing to do instead of acting on your dream. You may not hire that person because you believe things are easier if you just do them yourself.

I'm not saying you have to make a million dollars to call yourself a success. However, no matter what level you want to take yourself, there are times you may just be holding your own self back to get there.

Here is a perfect example of this. I just recently found someone selling services for the exact thing that I need right now. I've known her for a while, but she recently launched this specific piece to her business. I was ecstatic when she announced she was doing it and immediately reached out to her.

I heard nothing back.

So I reached out to her a second way, and I finally got a response. We set up an initial meeting, and honestly I just had to run a couple of things by her before I signed the dotted line. This wasn't going to be a hard sell for her at all. Then about 30 minutes before our meeting, she cancelled on me. She had something come up unexpectedly and needed to reschedule. The only problem is, she never rescheduled, and I haven't heard from her since.

As excited I was to work with her, there is a line I draw as to how much I'm going to beg you to take my money. I have no idea what is going on in her world, but this has self-sabotage written all over it.

Another example of seeing others self-sabotage was a few years ago when I was working on remodeling one of my rentals. It happened to be in another state, and I made arrangements to be there for a weekend to meet with potential contractors. I lined up ten different interviews to get estimates. Two people showed up, and only one of them ended up providing an estimate. I don't believe there were nine contractors who couldn't use the business.

I recently did this myself. I had an amazing speaking opportunity pretty much handed to me. In order to make it happen, I had to turn in one document. I was scared to create this document because I had to make myself sound pretty amazing. I was afraid I wasn't going to live up to the hype, and so instead of pushing through it, I sat on it. I sat on it for two months. I made the creator of the event so angry that they told me I was out. He thought I was snubbing him and not appreciative of the opportunity.

I was so appreciative of the opportunity that I didn't feel I could live up to it. Luckily, an apology on my end made things right.

However, this is the perfect picture of how self-sabotage can contribute immensely to whether or not we succeed.

We have all been there. We know we need to write that email, but we just never do it. We know we should reach out to that one person who has the potential make a huge difference, but we hold back. We have a customer waiting to give us business, but for some reason we mess it up.

There are psychological factors at play with this, too; that can unfold from childhood. We hold subconscious beliefs of what we believe we deserve of success. When we start to get close to that level, we do something to bring us back down.

These beliefs can stem from so many things. Were you told as a child not to take chances that could potentially hurt you? Were you told always to be modest? Have you been told or ever told yourself 'who do you think you are?' Have you held yourself back because of where you came from; believing no one from that situation could ever make anything of themselves? As unimportant as these might seem, they are all limiting beliefs that are controlling your actions today.

So even though success is on your radar, and you feel that, yes, this is exactly what you want, start looking at what might be holding you back. I love this quote by Marianne Williamson:

> 'Our deepest fear is not that we are inadequate. Our deepest fear is that we are powerful beyond measure. It is our light, not our darkness that most frightens us. We ask ourselves, who am I to be brilliant, gorgeous, talented, fabulous? Actually,

who are you NOT to be? You are a child of God. Your playing small does not serve the world. There is nothing enlightened about shrinking so that other people won't feel insecure around you. We are all meant to shine, as children do. We were born to make manifest the glory of God that is within us. It's not just in some of us; it's in everyone. And as we let our own light shine, we unconsciously give other people permission to do the same. As we are liberated from our own fear, our presence automatically liberates others.'

A fantastic reminder is to once again, allow yourself to believe this is all possible, and that it is yours for the taking. You can't hold yourself back scared that someone may take it from you, or in fear that you may get all you want.

It's your job to share these talents with the world. Put yourself out there!

If it makes you feel better, I have many more examples of self-sabotage. I had a huge problem procrastinating. Even with this book. I was so close to being done, but putting that 'final' status on it, was too terrifying. I did some visualization and discovered that I was terrified of letting people down. I was also terrified of letting myself down. Putting this book out to the world was everything to me. It was something I had dreamed of for a long time. I made it mean so much that I was scared it was going to fail.

It wasn't only about this book, but my online programs, too. I was scared to sell my programs. What if someone bought them, and then decided they didn't get their money's worth? I had worked with so many people who had over-delivered, that I was afraid I wouldn't live up to those same standards.

It was easier to be three-quarters of the way finished and never to have to let anyone down. The only problem was that I was letting someone down. I was letting myself down.

I knew I was dragging my feet and self-sabotaging. And I had no good reason. Finally coming to that realization was an eye opener for me. Instead of concentrating on the fear, I concentrated on doing the best I absolutely could do. That best still may disappoint some people, but at least I was giving it my all.

If you are struggling with this, then I would encourage you to start doing some inner work. Start noticing how you feel when you envision yourself successful. What feelings are you suddenly aware of that weren't there before? Being open to this will help you tremendously when it comes to getting yourself over these hurdles.

I also can't stress enough to *not* think this doesn't apply to you. We all have some limiting beliefs. I wish I had learned about these in my twenties, heck even in high school. I had put so many limitations on myself about how far I would go in life that I held myself back for far too long.

Life is too short, and yes, you may let a few people down along the way. However, the last place you want to be is at the end of your life, wishing you would have followed through.

Chapter 8

Research Your Idea

Now that I've mentally prepared you for all that entrepreneurship entails, and how to set yourself up for the most success, it's time to get into a little bit of meat.

As I have mentioned, it's crucial that you have a product or service that someone actually will want to purchase. You'll need to figure out:

o   Are your services needed?

o   Do they solve a problem?

o   Are they something people are willing to pay money for?

As you navigate these questions and decide if you should make a business out of your idea, the first question you should ask is: *'Will this product or service add value?'*

I talk about that question a lot. I honestly feel if you can go through life with a direction of service and a direction of value, anything is possible. Too many people jump in to make money without first asking themselves the important questions.

Step 1. In putting together a business plan, first figure out something that will truly add value to the world. Can you make peoples' lives easier? Can you make the world a better place? Just saying 'yes' to these two questions will put you leaps and bounds above the rest.

Step 2. The second thing I need you to do when researching your business is to make sure you know who your ideal client is. Please don't start a business saying your product or service will help everyone. As in: 'I have this 'Healthy For You Item' and it will help everyone with a body who wants to be healthier!' I see that type of unrealistic scope far too often. Answers like this are way too broad.

Your ideal client should not consist of the word 'body': everybody, somebody, or anybody.

Most businesses make their ideal client too broad because they are afraid they're going to miss out on potential business. They feel that marketing too specifically will make them lose out on business. There are several popular quotes that address this for a reason. Like 'jack of all trades, master of none.' Or 'If you try to appeal to everyone, you'll appeal to no one.' These are all very simple terms with very profound statements behind them.

Let me give you a perfect example. I do a lot of work with chiropractors, and let me tell you, this is one of the most difficult groups to make narrow their focus, or niche down. I mean after all, they help everyone who has a spine, right?

However, I hate to be harsh, but where I live you can pretty much find a chiropractor on every corner. Since they all help people who have a spine, it becomes more crucial to niche down and be specific about who they serve. I encourage them to think about the pain or problem their potential client is going through when they start to need their service. What kind of conversation will they be having with someone? What will they be searching for on Google?

If they help anybody who wants to be healthier (I hear this one all the time at networking events), it doesn't mean anything to anybody because I have no idea what that even means. Are they sick and dying and need to be healthier? Are they overweight and struggling with losing weight? Are they relatively healthy just looking for that extra push? Being healthier could mean so many things. No one says I want to be healthier because they are usually looking for something more specific.

As an example, what if the message changed to 'I help women who are in their late 30's and early 40's, who are doing everything right, but still can't lose weight?' That simple statement on who they help changes everything.

As a woman in this situation, I'm annoyed that I can't lose weight. I'm searching specific things trying to find out what is going on with my body. I'm having conversations with friends telling them this specific thing. When I say I'm struggling with this, they can immediately say 'I know the perfect person you need to see.'

You have to niche down and stop trying to do what everyone else is doing. You don't want to be like everyone else. You want to stand out. The way you can do that is by understanding your ideal client so well that you speak their language. They know you get them, and there no longer is any question to them on whether they should buy from you or not. Their minds are already made up.

When you're just like everyone else, there's nothing about you that makes you different. When you do what everyone else does, you're a dime a dozen.

So if I'm your patient or even a networking partner, how can I sell you to others? There is nothing special that you do outside from everyone else. Maybe all I can say is that you're really good. Most times, though, that doesn't go too far.

The niche can be one of your most incredible steps in building your business, even if it feels like it will do the opposite. The niche helps you become 'that guy' or 'that girl.' The one you HAVE to see or buy from based on the problem your product or service solves. No, I may not recommend you to everyone you could potentially help. But when someone needs that particular thing you specialize in, that referral becomes entirely different. I have an intention behind it. The story changes from 'hey, I know someone who might be able to help you' to 'I have someone you've got to see. They specialize in this!'

If you were a person listening to those recommendations, there is no hesitation to seek out this business. That is exactly what a niche does. In that moment of referral, you go from the 'I think you should' to 'you HAVE to.'

Knowing your ideal client is crucial. If you think your business is to serve everyone with a <fill-in a very general need here> who breaths, who has a body, who wants a better life, who (the vague answers could continue) you're not going to go anywhere. Hone down, understand completely and fully who your ideal client is. Niche, connect, and find out what problems they are experiencing. It's then up to you to define how your product or service solves those problems.

It is okay if you have a couple of types of clients who you help. But get to know both of them. Why is this important? Your marketing message is going to change for each of them, so to connect you need to make sure you're putting out the right message. You can't just put out a blanket message to succeed. They have to feel like you're talking directly to them, and you're the one who is going to help them with a particular problem.

Let me give you an example. One of my courses is called The Prestigious Practice. The original intent was to put the course in front of chiropractic students. As I rolled out my first version, I found that not only was this course helpful to them, I had a ton of doctors who had been practicing for several years asking for help, too.

When it came time to launch the second version of my course, I knew the program could help both demographics. However, connecting to them needed to happen separately. So when I created my promo videos, I made sure to create two: one that spoke to students, and one that spoke to doctors. It was the same product, just different marketing.

I also had to run completely different Facebook Ads. I first tried to run the same picture within the ad to the different groups, but just with different copy. However, I wasn't converting well at all with the students. I not only had to make the copy different, but I had to use an image of a younger person in order to get a better conversion for that ad. Knowing the smallest details of your business can make the biggest impact.

Step 3. Once you've figured out whom you want to target, find them. Facebook Groups or Google+ Communities are the first two places I would search. Finding them is important for two reasons. First, it allows you to connect. There is no greater data than being able to talk to your ideal client. Find out if the product or service you're putting together is something they even need.

Second, this will allow you to know their language. Putting their language in your marketing will be huge for the success and growth of your business. You will also want to see how they speak. You will want to find out what they find frustrating, or where they need the most help. Sure, you could guess at all these things, but why waste the time hoping you're right? Why not take the extra effort to make sure you are on the EXACT path, not just a path you think might be right?

I see many people at this stage in their business make a pretty big mistake. They are afraid of sharing their idea for fear someone is going to steal it. The truth is, it's more likely someone already has your idea (and I'll get to that in a moment). What you need to do is make yourself different or better, find a need that isn't being met. And you need to run like hell to market. You won't be the first, and you don't want to be the last. It is just more motivation for you to move! It's not the idea that matters, it is the execution of the idea that will make or break your business.

Sharing with and asking your ideal customers gives you far richer data than you could ever pay for. As you're talking to people, don't say this is what I'm thinking, would you pay 'X' for it? Simply ask them, this is what I'm thinking. First, would you use this product/service? Hopefully, the answer is yes, and once they say yes, then ask them what they would pay for it. Make sure you understand that question. It's not would you pay 'X' for it, but what would you pay for it? Value is very important in what you're offering. You need to make sure your ideal customer sees the value in it, and the only way you're going to find that out is by asking.

Another great tip for finding out what your customer needs, and what they're looking for, is by using Google Adwords [see below]. Not only will you get the number of searches per topic, but you can get other ideas around what exactly they're searching. It gives you the opportunity to 'see more like this' and it will give you a ton of insight into what people are actually searching for and the number of searches behind them.

If no one is searching for what you're about to build a business around, it is probably a good idea to take a step back and do a little more research to make sure this is something people actually need. Taking these few extra steps will be crucial to getting you where you need to be.

How exactly do you use Google Keywords? Go to https://www.google.com/adwords/. You will need a Gmail account to do this, and first, fill out your business information. On the second page, you can go to the Keywords Section to start doing some research. In this example, I initially searched for 'how to start a business'. Google is showing how many people search for this topic in the location I selected (which is the United States and Canada). Then you can continue to click 'more like this', where Google will continue to give you ideas.

Start typing in your first keyword or phrase, and let Google start doing the work for you. Here's a picture of what the area looks like.

Keywords	Add around 15-20 keywords.			
	These are the search terms that may trigger your ad to appear next to search results.			

Keyword	Search popularity ?		
how to start a business	90500	More like this	×
starting a business	40500		×
start a business	9900		×
steps to starting a business	2900		×
starting a small business	9900		×
starting a business uk	880		×
starting an online business	5400		×
start an online business	1600		×
how to start online business	4400		×
start online business	1600		×

Enter keywords separated by commas **Add**

Save Cancel

This is a great starting point to see if your product or service is in demand. Continue to play with various keywords and use the 'more like this button' to get new ideas. Something may pop up that you hadn't even thought of. I recommend making a spreadsheet to track the keywords along with the search numbers. You will also start using this in the next chapter when you start defining what makes you stand out.

If you want to get a little more technical and in-depth, you can take the Google Keyword Planner Tool a step further. You do have to act like you are opening an account with them and put your credit card on file. However, you never have to give them any money in order to get this data.

Once your account is set-up, go to the Google Keyword Planner Tool, and then look to Find New Keywords. Type in your keyword, your area, etc, and you will end up with something like this:

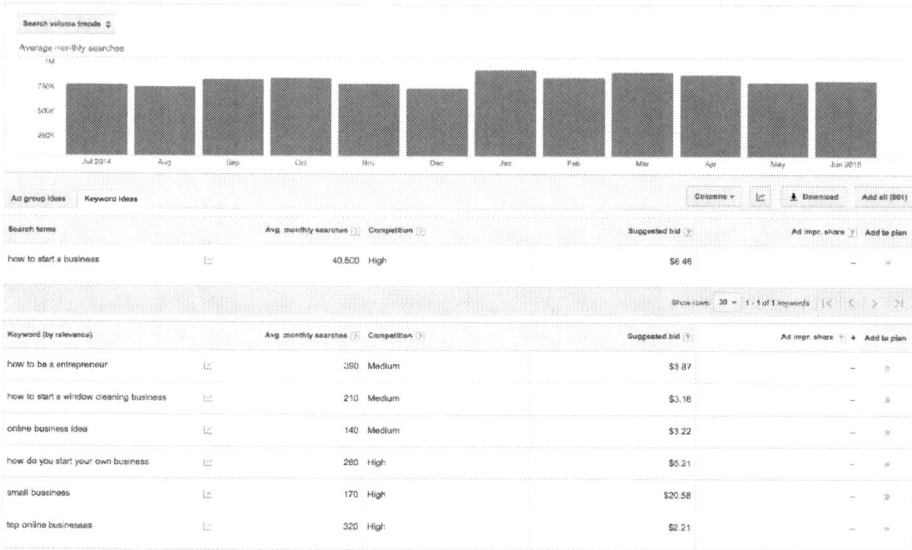

Search terms		Avg. monthly searches	Competition	Suggested bid		Ad impr. share	Add to plan
how to start a business		40,500	High	$6.46		--	»

Keyword (by relevance)		Avg. monthly searches	Competition	Suggested bid		Ad impr. share	Add to plan
how to be a entrepreneur		390	Medium	$3.87		--	»
how to start a window cleaning business		210	Medium	$3.18		--	»
online business idea		140	Medium	$3.22		--	»
how do you start your own business		260	High	$5.21		--	»
small business		170	High	$20.58		--	»
top online businesses		320	High	$2.21		--	»

This is a lot more detail and insight into one search term along with ideas for other related terms. This will help you understand other things people might be searching for, along with the number of searches for each. The competition column lets you see how much competition you have of people bidding (Google AdWords) on particular terms, and the suggested bid is also Google AdWords related.

Again, start tracking these terms because it will start allowing you to see if there is a need for your product or service. It will also get you ready to start defining where you stand out.

Chapter 9

Define What Will Make You Stand Out

This is so important to your business because not only will you need to determine this to help share with others what makes you stand out. It will also create more confidence in you as you begin to sell your products and services.

There are two aspects to figuring out this piece of your business. The first is to own who you are and why you have the right to charge money. This may sound simple, but so many people never do this.

Before you get any further in this book, I want you to stop and write down five things that make you stand out above the rest. Yes, this is before you start checking out your competition. You have aligned yourself with this potential business for a reason, and now it's time to own that.

If it takes you a long time to come up with five, or if you are hesitant in any way while writing these down, I want you to do this every single day. I want you do it until it becomes second nature and until you can say what you do with confidence.

You have every right to be in this business, and you have every right to sell a product or service. We will talk about your positioning in a moment, and figuring out how to price things. However, no matter where you set your prices, understand you must own your expertise and your knowledge.

Now let's talk about finding your competitive edge, and how you will position your business compared to others.

As you start getting into researching, you are more than likely going to find someone already doing what you were hoping to do. Before you get angry when you see someone already has your idea and is running with it, stop. Please don't throw in the towel because let me assure you this is a good thing.

Yes, it's a good thing. It means someone is already making money doing what you want to do. It means there is a market for it. Next, it's highly doubtful that one person can help every single person who needs this service. If it happens to be a product, maybe there's something missing in their product that with a little more thought or work on your end, could end up blowing theirs out of the water.

For example, what happens if you used Hertz, and they totally upset you, but they were the only one out there? You would be stuck with them. Isn't it a beautiful thing that we get options?

If you're a soda drinker, aren't you happy Pepsi or Dr. Pepper didn't sit out because Coke was already on the market? Or think of your favorite Italian restaurant. What if they had said there's already an Italian restaurant within driving distance so we probably shouldn't open one? I'm not telling you to open something across the street. But don't sit back and say because someone has already done it, that you're not allowed to. Put your own spin on it.

What if Starbucks had never jumped in the ring because Dunkin' Donuts already sold coffee? A life without Starbucks is a life I never want to imagine.

So if you find out someone already is doing what you want to do, here is your next step. Instead of giving up, I want you to find what it is exactly they're offering. Create a spreadsheet and track the following:

- What they're charging
- How they're trying to position themselves
- What specifically they're contributing
- Who they are serving
- Their price points
- How they are adding value outside of the product
- Their background and expertise, etc.

See if there is other competition out there and continue to work through this exercise to find out how you can differentiate yourself.

If you need help trying to figure out if you do have competitors, take those Google Search Terms we looked up in the previous chapter. Then start typing them in to find out what websites are coming up.

This will give you some great insight into what others are already doing.

Track their marketing strategies, and guess as much as you can whom they're targeting. Is their market exactly like yours, or could you put another spin on it? Google them and read comments about them. Do people love them? If so, what do they love? Have they complained? If so, what have they complained about? Continue to use all these tools to think about ways you can make your product or service better.

You can also improve a product or service by thinking about community and your tribe. This is a big one. Everyone loves community. If you can create a deeper community among your followers and customers, you will be off to a great start. Check out what your competitors are already doing and figure out a way you can do it better.

Now this is where you start blending your top five qualities with how you can stand out. Take your strengths and ask yourself how you compare to these other companies. Are you more experienced than the people who have called themselves experts? Don't panic if not. Once again, you're different, and that may be all you need.

It is important to understand, this is not the place for copying. This is super important. I mentioned this before, but I really want to drive this point home. Don't, absolutely don't, copy other peoples' work. You are you, and if you're going to make yourself different, you better be the one creating the content, including writing, recording, etc. If you're trying to be someone else, people will read through that almost immediately, and you won't be able to keep up the act forever.

Here is the great thing about people and connections. The more someone gets to know you, the more they are either going to really like you or decide they don't like you. You might be wondering, *not like me, how is that good?* But wouldn't you rather connect with someone who loves what you're about and what you do and is a raving fan? Then you can get the haters or the indifferent people out of the way.

I love to correlate this to dating. When I was in my twenties, I was pretty insecure. If I liked a guy, I wanted him to like me. I would compromise who I was if it meant getting him to like me. For example, if you talk to me for as little as two minutes, you will 100% understand how independent I am, and how important that is to me. However, in my twenties I met a Greek Pilot. The accent, the job … I won't get into it all, but he was pretty amazing. He was also pretty much a ladies man. But I turned the other cheek. I thought maybe I could stay at home while he traveled the world and likely had other women, too.

Yes, I thought that. I honestly, thought that. Looking back, I realize how crazy it was, but at the time, I really thought it might not be so bad.

Well, thank goodness we never ended up together. I did end up married to another man, and four years later, at thirty-two, I was divorced. I learned that changing and working overtime to make a connection that only traveled one way didn't do anyone any good.

After doing some soul searching, I started dating again in my thirties. I let go of my insecurities, and instead of trying to impress a guy because I liked him, I learned to say this is me, take me or leave me. I didn't pick them apart, and say 'well he needs to change this and that, and maybe this will work.' Either I accepted who they were, or I didn't, and the same happened for me. I ended up with probably one of the greatest guys I could find, all because I stopped trying to be what I thought people would want me to be.

You might be wondering how dating has anything to do with you and your business, but it's the same thing. You're courting customers, and if they feel you're telling them what they want to hear versus what you believe, they'll see right through you. Life is not just about relationships, but authentic ones. Work on building them not only in your life, but your business, too.

So just be you. Put yourself out there, be quirky if that's your thing, or be straight laced if that's your thing. You'll attract the right customers once you start putting the real you out there. Ignore the haters because you will never make everyone happy, so never let anyone like that question what you're doing.

I do want to talk about pricing for just a moment because I think it's critical to start thinking about this. As you start looking at what your competitors are doing, I want to make sure you're looking at what they are charging so you can figure out where your products or services fit in. I think you also should understand where the market is, so as you do your research, you can plan for profit margins, etc.

What I beg you not to do is to not make one of the things that stand out about you that you're cheaper than everyone else. Walmart already took that business model, so please don't grab it for yourself.

If being the cheapest is what will make you stand out from the rest, your business will fade quickly. Even if you think you're doing it to build your business, it doesn't quite work that way. You only attract the cheap customers and take it from me, those are not the ones you want to work with. There is never a moment in time, where they value so much of what you're doing, that they want to pay you more money for the same product or service. Instead, they will drain you as they try to get as much value out of you as possible.

When you're starting out, I get it will be harder to compete with businesses and people who have been around longer. However, instead of going cheaper, just figure out a way to add more value. Don't run yourself ragged, working with bad clients essentially for free.

Own what makes you stand out, and why you can charge what you feel you are worth, and charge that! Yes, it might be hard at first when you are starting to build your business. However, I promise as your business begins to grow, you will thank me.

Define what gives you a right to do what you want to be doing, and own that. Then combine that knowledge with putting your spin on things, and you'll soon have a business that not only stands out but is making lots of money!

Chapter 10

Put It All Together

I think I should tell you upfront, this is NOT a chapter that is going to give you all of the answers. Or possibly any of the answers. Except maybe one: You don't have to have all of the answers starting out, you simply have to be willing to learn.

One of the very first pieces you are going to need to learn and start figuring out is what this is all going to cost, funding, etc. This is one of the biggest parts that trip people up. Before you start asking how to do that, I want you to sit down and start calculating what you really need. Start asking yourself questions like:

- Will you have to hire people, and if so, how many?
- What will their salaries be?
- Will you require office space/real estate?
- How much lead time will you need to get everything running?
- Do you have a physical product? If so, what will it take to start manufacturing?

Start laying out piece by piece everything you're going to need to put this business together. No, you are not going to know everything, but start putting together as much as possible. Then when you get stuck find out where you need to get the answer or whom you need to talk to. For example, if you are trying to figure out what real estate will cost, contact a realtor who specializes in commercial property. They will help you in your research. Find out what office buildings will cost, and what you will need to begin.

Your business plan will ultimately be determined based on how much money you're going to need and who will be investing. I'm embarrassed to say this, but I never had a business plan for my first business. I also never needed anyone to give me money to build it.

I would suggest you start laying out your goals, what you want to make from it, etc. Then lay out what you feel your initial products and services will be, how much you will charge, and how much they will cost to make. Start working your way backwards. If you don't require an investor, your business plan could be a simple document about what your business is about, what you plan to sell, and how you plan to take your product or service to market. If you will require more financing, it is going to need to be something more elaborate.

With every new portion of your business that comes, you will soon discover that you are going to need to start with what you know and figure out the rest. It's kind of like the 'how do you eat an elephant' analogy; take one bite at a time.

I know one of the biggest things that stopped me and many others in their entrepreneurial journey is that we didn't have all the answers. Furthermore, it's not one answer for one question. There are many, many questions.

Instead of finding those answers, the easy way out is to give up.

I have good news and bad news for you in this. Let me go ahead and give the bad news first: You will never have the answers to everything. And honestly, is that really a shock to you? If you're a parent when that baby entered this world, did you have the answers to everything? Maybe you're a few years in, now do you have all of the answers?

Has there ever been a week of your life, in any or every aspect of your life, when you had all of the answers? You get my point. We never have them. So why is it when a great idea appears in our head, we suddenly say, 'well I can't do it because I don't have all of the answers?'

With other things become important enough to you, you have managed to figure out some of the answers. Those same rules apply in business. When you decide to stop being afraid and decide that this business is important enough to follow through with, you'll start finding the answers you need. You simply have to start looking.

I have some more bad news. Instead of getting an answer and being done with things, getting a question answered will probably lead to a hundred more questions.

Let's use marketing as an example. When you start, one of your first steps is to find out the best way to market your business. You do some research, and you ask around and discover that the best step for you to take might be to get into Facebook Ads. Then your next question becomes 'How do I run a Facebook Ad?'

The good news is that because you are asking all of the questions, you'll learn more being an entrepreneur than you would ever learn at any other company you've worked for.

You become a pro at many things, and you meet other people who will help you with the things you don't know. Doesn't it sound a little exciting now?

In the five years I owned my first business, here are just a few things off the top of my head that I learned:

- How to build a website and basic SEO
- How to create a blog
- How to market/Google Ads/Networking
- How to hire employees and contractors and the difference between them
- How to work with your spouse (actually didn't learn that one as we ended up divorced, but I had a ton of lessons learned for the next relationship)
- Employee policy and procedures – how to create them and why they're crucial in your business
- How to buy and sell a business (I wrote my own contract when I sold it)

I knew NONE, not a one of these things when I started my business. I just learned as I went. If something came up that left me clueless, I didn't quit. I asked, or I read a book, or I went on our good friend Mr. Google and asked him the question.

I want you to understand you don't have to be brilliant; you simply have to be willing to learn. You have to be willing to put in the long nights and days.

I hope you're realizing you actually can do this, and you actually WILL do this (and yes, there is a big difference). You need to put it all together figure out if your product and service is viable and to see how what you want to do in a business fits within the marketplace. … And then what?

First things first, you need to change your language. Talk the talk. No more with the 'thinking you want to do this' or 'you are trying a new business' or 'you think you might like this thing.' Nope, you ARE doing this. Talk like you're doing it and start telling people you are doing it. The more you hide behind 'maybes', the more likely the chances of it never getting off the ground. Start moving forward, and start making it happen.

Not only will this change your mindset, but it will open doors for you. I'm huge into networking, and when I start talking about what I'm doing putting it out there, people are excited. They become eager to connect me with the people that they know who could help me, and then everything starts getting in motion. Networking will be one of the greatest assets in your business, and you'll never get there if you keep your new business to yourself.

Second, start referring to yourself as an entrepreneur. Start thinking like one. So many times, especially when we are moonlighting, this is a side thing. We may not be making enough money and may feel like an imposture for calling ourselves an entrepreneur. I spent so many years comparing myself to the Donald Trumps and Mark Cubans of the world and wondered how I could ever possibly compare?

I finally allowed myself to compare because even though I don't have the companies the size of theirs, I still hustled. I went from an idea and started a business from it. That alone is a bigger step than most people will make in their lifetime. Just by taking those steps forward, you have every right in the world to label yourself as an entrepreneur.

Do your research, taking it all one step at a time. If you keep looking at everything that needs to be done, you will get overwhelmed. If you concentrate on taking one positive step every day toward your goal, each day you will get one step closer to your dreams. It may seem like a large undertaking at the beginning, but you will get there, I promise.

Try to go in with as little cost as you can, and then slowly build your company that way. The last place you want to be is where you feel desperate for sales. Don't jump in too far over your head.

I say this because so many people think it's going to take too much money to begin, and so they stop before they even begin. They never dig deep to look at the numbers and discover what it is going to take. They only assume they can't afford it, or it is going to take too much so they never try.

Now no more hoping, wishing, and wondering. It's time to get to it!

If you want some more steps in setting up your business visit http://thestartersclub.com/10_Business_Steps for some free resources.

About the Author

Unlike many refugees from Corporate America, Erin Smith had never thought about being her own boss. While rising up the ranks of the VUI world (Voice User Interface), she was soon speaking at conventions, being quoted in industry magazines, and quickly working her way up the corporate ladder. However, her life changed when she read, "Rich Dad, Poor Dad" and embraced the concept of owning.

After investing in real estate across the country, Erin and her husband started a pet sitting business called Amore Pet Care. She took the company from an idea to selling it five years later with a six-figure income, 12 employees and a large client list, all while keeping her corporate job.

Erin's next venture was The Sunless Diva, a mobile spray tanning business, spurred by her desire to have someone spray tan her at her house, since skin cancer runs in her family. Again, Erin built the business from scratch and within a year, added several employees and at one point operated out of six salons.

Her success with starting, building and selling small businesses led Erin to create The Starters Club, an online business providing courses and coaching for would-be and new entrepreneurs.

A busy mom of two toddlers, Erin holds a Bachelor of Science (BS), Management Information Systems from the University of Wisconsin - Eau Claire.